Praise for *The 60-Second Shrink*

"To impart wisdom comprehensively and understandably is a formidable task; to do so succinctly as well is nothing short of miraculous. The Drs. Lazarus have tackled over 100 difficult life situations that are common to all of us. The strategies imparted in The 60-Second Shrink *are profound, yet practical and workable insights which are a lot less expensive than a fifty-minute shrink. Seldom can something so solution focused be also so entertaining. The first time the reader picks it up he or she will discover it is almost impossible to put it down. It is must reading for everyone who wants to remain 'sane in a crazy world,' and after the initial encounter the reader will be referring to it over and over again for many years."*

---- Nicholas A. Cummings, Ph.D., Sc.D.
President, Foundation for Behavioral Health, and
Former President of the American Psychological Association

"Find yourself in this book and find yourself better! Lazarus and Lazarus, internationally-renowned psychotherapists, provide an eminently readable distillation of common problems and practical pointers to help you reclaim your life."

---- Jeffrey K. Zeig, Ph.D.
Director, The Milton Erickson Foundation

"The 60-Second Shrink *is chock full of valuable suggestions and helpful advice. It's amazing how much useful information is contained in this slim volume. The book belongs in every home in America."*

---- Bernie Zilbergeld, Ph.D.
Author of *Male Sexuality* and *The New Male Sexuality*

"The 60-Second Shrink *is an incredibly clever and informative self-help book that offers a tremendous amount of sound advice on a host of common human emotional problems (or troubles). This book, authored by two renowned psychologists, is scientifically accurate, up-to-date, and very reader-friendly. I recommend it highly."*

---- John Preston, Psy.D.
Author of *You Can Beat Depression* and *Every Session Counts*

ARNOLD A. LAZARUS, PH.D.
CLIFFORD N. LAZARUS, PH.D.

THE 60-SECOND SHRINK

101 Strategies
For Staying Sane in a Crazy World

Impact Publishers®

SAN LUIS OBISPO, CALIFORNIA 93406

Impact Publishers and colophon are registered trademarks of Impact Publishers, Inc.

ATTENTION ORGANIZATIONS AND CORPORATIONS:
This book is available at quantity discounts on bulk purchases for educational, business, or sales promotional use. For further information, please contact Impact Publishers, P.O. Box 1094, San Luis Obispo, CA 93406 (Phone: 1-800-2-IMPACT).

Library of Congress Cataloging-in-Publication Data

Lazarus, Arnold A.
    The 60-second shrink : 101 strategies for staying sane in a crazy
world / Arnold A. Lazarus, Clifford N. Lazarus.
        p.   cm.
    Includes bibliographical references and index.
    ISBN 1-886230-04-8 (alk. paper)
        1. Conduct of life.   2. Mental health—Popular works.
    I. Lazarus, Clifford N., 1961-   .   II. Title.
    BF637.C5L392   1997
    158—dc21   96-53590
                                                                      CIP

Publisher's Note

This publilcation is designed to provide accurate and authoritative information in regard to the subject matter covered. It is sold with the understanding that the publisher is not engaged in rendering psychological, medical, or other professional services. If expert assistance or counseling is needed, the services of a competent professional should be sought.

Printed in the United States of America on acid-free paper
Cover design by Sharon Schnare, San Luis Obispo, California

Published by *Impact Publishers*®
POST OFFICE BOX 1094
SAN LUIS OBISPO, CALIFORNIA 93406

Contents

FOREWORD

I first met Arnold and Clifford Lazarus in 1970 when I was a psychiatric resident at Yale University Medical School. Arnold was then a Visiting Professor and Director of Clinical Training in the Department of Psychology at Yale University, and I baby-sat for nine-year-old Clifford and his eleven-year-old sister Linda. Back then, Cliff was into flying kites, launching water-powered rocket ships, and getting into mischief, but it was quite evident that he was a very smart kid. It has been fascinating to observe the degree of eminence that Arnold has achieved and to watch his son Clifford sail through his doctorate in clinical psychology and proceed, metaphorically speaking, to stand on his father's shoulders rather than follow in his footsteps. In addition to obtaining a good grounding in psychotherapy, Clifford spent about five years heading up a research team in a psychiatric facility that was dedicated to evaluating new generation psychiatric medications, and he also became proficient at Neuro-psychological testing.

As is evident throughout this extremely informative and delightful book, the Drs. Lazarus have a talent for distilling complex material into very understandable prose. It is most important to demystify the fields of psychology, psychiatry and mental health in general, and my own books reflect this quest. It is amazing how much useful information has been so neatly packaged into this slim volume. This father-and-son team have a talent for cutting to the chase, for finding lucid ways of expressing their views, and for coming up with advice, which if followed, can only enhance the quality of life.

What I like most is how easy it is to read this engaging book. Sections can be skimmed through or thoroughly perused without having to wade through long, tedious or ponderous material (which unfortunately is true for far too many books!). In every instance, the message is there — right up front. The gems of wisdom scattered throughout are such that virtually everyone will find interesting information that can often be put to good personal use. Father and son have compiled a number of tools for keeping you and your loved ones in top mental health. This treasure trove is a must for your family bookshelf, to be used over and over again. I hope this charming book will be widely read.

— Harold H. Bloomfield, M.D.
Author of the best-selling *How to Heal Depression*

INTRODUCTION

As co-hosts of a weekly hour-long, call-in talk show that Clifford named Mental Health Matters (broadcast out of Princeton, New Jersey AM radio station, 1350 WHWH), we were requested to present a "mental health matter" to be aired on Mondays through Fridays as part of the daily 5 p.m. - 6 p.m. news hour. The idea of providing succinct and straightforward mental health tips and highlighting other aspects of psychology and psychiatry seemed appealing. Whereas our weekly show called for little preparation (especially when we had an eloquent guest on the program, or when callers raised interesting issues), the daily "mental health matters" had to be written out and carefully scripted. We would each compose three or four and then record them at the studio, taking turns to read alternating paragraphs. Putting together these tips, topics and vignettes required significant time and thought, and when several friends and listeners suggested that it might be very worthwhile to publish them, we decided to go ahead and give it a try.

Readers will find some repetitive material in several segments. This is because the items were presented on the air in a different order from that outlined in the book. We had considered editing out recurrent themes but changed our minds because by emphasizing and re-emphasizing important facts, it is likely that they will have a greater impact.

We like books that don't have to be read from cover to cover but readily lend themselves to selective browsing. THE 60-SECOND SHRINK can be scanned in any order. It is easy to skim through various sections and pick out specific parts that may interest you. The brief commentaries are intended to provide easily accessible food for thought, helpful hints and worthwhile vignettes. We are most grateful to Susan Krieger who kindly read through the entire manuscript and offered many helpful suggestions.

We genuinely hope that this little book contains material that most people will find informative and helpful. As far as we know, there is nothing quite like it on the market, and we hope that the printed word will permit us to reach an audience far beyond the boundaries of Central New Jersey. The views expressed are not necessarily those of the management of WHWH-AM Princeton.

STRATEGIES FOR STAYING SANE

1. What to Say When You Talk to Yourself

❖

Charlene was very hard on herself and often put herself down. While she'd never dream of verbally abusing or even harshly criticizing others, she nevertheless thought it was perfectly acceptable to treat herself in this manner. So, while other people thought well of her and seemed to like her very much, Charlene couldn't understand why she felt unhappy most of the time and suffered from low self-esteem.

❖

We talk to ourselves more or less continuously. Our brains are always active and a lot of what they do is tell us about ourselves. This "self-talk" takes place silently, of course, in the privacy of our minds.

Just like statements that come from other people, our inner statements can affect us dramatically. Unfortunately, many people give themselves a hard time by talking to themselves in harsh and unkind ways, perhaps because critical parents, teachers and others have led them to believe many negative things about themselves. Are you among these self-critical individuals?

Self-talk, for an unfortunately large number of people, consists of telling themselves what's wrong with them. They often repeat such statements as, "I'm stupid," "I'm selfish," "I sound like a fool," "I always manage to say the wrong thing," "I'm a complete failure," and other self-defeating phrases.

And it gets worse. We've had clients whose main message to themselves was, "You're such an idiot, such a total incompetent that you don't deserve to be the least bit happy."

Negative self-talk will usually lead to anxiety and depression and can have other unfortunate results. Self-fulfilling prophecies are quite common:

You start believing your own propaganda and bring about what you fear. (See "Self-Fulfilling Prophecies and Negativity Cycles," and "More about Self-Fulfilling Prophecies.")

Happily, the converse is also true. Positive self-talk will tend to achieve desirable outcomes and generate good feelings. When faced with a difficult situation, Harriet says, "It's hopeless and I can't stand it!" Glenda says, "There's no reason to get upset. I'll take it easy, step by step, and I'll probably do just fine." The difference in attitude is obvious. Glenda has a much greater chance of success because of her positive outlook.

Does it help to change what you say to yourself? It sure does. Tell yourself often enough that you'll fail and you almost certainly will. Tell yourself often enough that you'll succeed and you greatly improve your chances of fulfillment and satisfaction.

- **Talk to yourself of past successes, of times you've done really well, of times you've overcome obstacles, of times you've felt good.**

Just as you felt good then, you can feel good now. Just as you overcame adversity then, you can overcome adversity now.

It's probably true that most successful people have failed more times than others simply because they've tried more things. Abraham Lincoln twice failed in business and lost seven elections for various offices. But he kept believing in himself and in what he wanted to do.

Successful people...

- **don't focus on failures (there's no point in doing so),**
- **see mistakes as learning experiences for growth and understanding,**
- **don't indulge in self-recrimination.**

Remember, the difference between the foolish and the wise, is not that the wise do not make mistakes. Rather it is that the wise *learn* from their mistakes instead of telling themselves they're stupid for making them. The bottom line:

"Say unto yourself what you would have others say unto you."

❖   ❖   ❖

2. The Power of Imagery

❖

Bill and Bob were good friends for many years who met while starting out as entry-level employees at a large corporation. They both developed an interest in golf and would play together regularly. Over the years, Bob seemed to enjoy more frequent promotions than Bill and his golf handicap improved faster than Bill's, too. When Bill asked Bob to what he attributed his success, Bob answered with one word, "visualization."

❖

Not everyone can picture scenes and events in their minds as clearly as photographs, but we all possess the ability to conjure up images with varying degrees of clarity. For example, if someone asks you how many windows are in your house, you will surely be able to form a picture of your house in your mind's eye and count them.

Everyone has heard about the power of positive thinking, but the power of *positive imaging* is even greater. In most cases, before you are capable of actually doing something, you first need to be able to picture yourself doing it.

Suppose you want to ask your boss for a raise. Can you visualize approaching him or her and asking for more money? Can you actually see yourself doing so? If your answer is "No," if you say "I can't imagine myself doing that," it is pretty obvious that you'll probably avoid the actual encounter ---- and you'll probably remain at your present salary.

On the other hand, if you can picture that scene, if you can see yourself calmly but assertively stating your case as to why you believe you deserve a higher wage, chances are that you will take action.

Many famous athletes choreograph their moves in imagery before going into action. For example, champion skiers imagine themselves negotiating almost every inch of a slope, champion tennis players picture themselves executing successful shots, and ballerinas and gymnasts will practice their moves as much in imagination as in actual rehearsal.

What we are getting at is very simple but extremely effective.

◆ **If you really wish to succeed at something, picture yourself doing it successfully over and over again.**

Obviously we are talking about visualizing success that lies within your reach. You will not succeed in doing the impossible no matter how much imagery you practice.

One of the most powerful methods is called *coping imagery*.

♦ **Picture yourself coping with difficult events. See yourself managing, perhaps struggling or battling, but nevertheless getting through it — attaining success.**

This exercise done repeatedly can enhance the likelihood of your actual success in many situations. What we are recommending, in effect, is *structured daydreaming*. Try it out and see what a difference it can make.

❖   ❖   ❖

3. Reprogramming Your Mind

❖

George had been an unhappy and anxious person for most of his adult life. Finally, after many years of silently watching him suffer, his younger sister, Jennie, suggested he seek counseling and disclosed to him that she had sought therapy some years ago and was greatly helped by it. "Oh, why bother," George remarked. "When you went for counseling you were young enough to benefit from it. I'm too old and set in my ways, and you can't teach an old dog new tricks."

❖

Most people assume that there is not much that can be done about the mind. If it shows you depressing pictures or dwells on discouraging thoughts, you go around feeling depressed.

If your mind keeps dwelling on inadequacies and faults, you'll go around feeling powerless and bad. If it keeps repeating that you can't do this and won't know that, you assume that's just how it is.

In fact, we can change and control our images and thoughts. People often say, "That's just the way I am." Untrue. It simply depends on who's in charge.

Minds do what they are programmed to do. Chances are that if you were belittled as a child, your mind will have recorded all those humiliations and will play them back at every opportunity. If you once had a bad experience with arithmetic, your mind may have decided to keep you away from anything having to do with numbers.

So here you are, ten, twenty, thirty or more years later, still telling yourself that you can't do math and making it impossible to give it a chance. Much of the mind's negative programming consists of such self-imposed limitations that keep you from realizing your potential.

But you don't have to be stuck with how your mind has been programmed.

+ **You can become your own programmer and manage your mind's productions.**

The different mind training methods are called by various names: mental practice, visualization, guided imagery, mindscripting, self-hypnosis, imagery rehearsal. We prefer the term *mental training* because you need to train your mind to get what you want.

Here is one of the most powerful mental training techniques. Most professional athletes do this routinely. Over and over again,

+ **picture yourself achieving something that really matters to you. Picture it vividly again and again.**

Chances become better and more likely that it will then happen to and for you.

Another powerful method of reprogramming your mind is to

+ **talk to your negative thoughts and pessimistic self-statements as if they were naughty children.**

Thus, the next time you put yourself down, for instance by saying something like "I'm stupid!" or "I'm such a weakling!" immediately address those statements — "Stop using words like 'stupid' or 'weak'! Shape up!" — and see what happens. You may be pleasantly surprised.

We recommend that you now read the next segment, "Achieving Mental Balance," and re-read "What to Say When You Talk to Yourself" (pages 1-2).

❖   ❖   ❖

4. Achieving Mental Balance

❖

Molly was described by her friends as a well-developed negative personality. "She's very good at seeing the dark side of things, but she does not often detect the positive aspects of her experiences," they observed. One of her friends actually called her "mentally lopsided," and wondered if there was some way for Molly to attain a more balanced outlook.

❖

While it is somewhat of an oversimplification, the brain can be thought of as being similar to a muscle. In the same way that muscles grow and become stronger through use and exercise, the brain also develops and changes through use and mental exertion.

Imagine what would happen if a weight lifter worked out much harder and longer with his or her right arm and pretty much neglected the left arm. Over time, the well-exercised right arm would be considerably firmer, larger, and stronger than the less exercised left arm.

Once this muscular imbalance or asymmetry develops, to balance his or her physique, the weight lifter will have to workout much more with the left arm than the right arm or the lopsidedness will never even out. So, for every one repetition of exercise the right arm does, the left will have to do two, three or more repetitions to eventually catch up.

In the brain, exercise is essentially thinking, visualizing, or any number of mental activities that stimulate parts of the brain and gets them working. Some recent evidence suggests that certain thoughts are governed by very specific brain structures and these structures develop and strengthen through use.

If someone frequently thinks negative, anxiety provoking, depressing or other psychologically stressful thoughts, it is probable that the areas governing these mental actions will strengthen through use thus increasing the likelihood of these undesirable thoughts occurring with greater force and frequency. Alternatively, different regions of the brain mediate more positive and neutral patterns of thinking and these areas, too, can be strengthened through use.

If you think you've been exercising your negative "mental muscles" too much

◆ **you can work to achieve greater mental balance by strengthening the positive mental regions,** just like you can strengthen a muscle through use and repetition.

♦ **For every negative thought, picture or idea that you have, try to entertain several positive or neutral alternatives.**

You want to catch yourself each time you make a negative statement or dwell on a pessimistic thought and immediately focus on several upbeat and cheerful perceptions.

Over time, this mental exercise will help to level the playing field and you'll enjoy the benefits of more balanced thinking.

❖   ❖   ❖

5. Exercising Your Brain

❖

Molly, whom we met in the previous vignette, doesn't know it, but she could employ several specific methods to better balance her perceptions. When a friend suggested some options for her, she said, "I'm satisfied being who I am. Besides, it's hard to change! So what if others are concerned?"

❖

Molly is right in one respect: It often takes some effort to attain mental equilibrium, just as it requires physical exercise to acquire and maintain a healthy body. But, as can been seen from the following account, there are methods that are straightforward and not difficult to implement.

Everyone knows that physical fitness benefits a lot from exercise. But how about mental fitness? Well, research has shown that physical fitness and emotional health go hand in hand. Cardiovascular benefits from exercise, for example, may help forestall degenerative changes in the brain. But let's talk specifically about exercising the brain or the mind.

Like good physical functioning, the essence of brain power is movement. Regular exercise, mental calisthenics, make the mind more alert and agile and ward off the aging process. There is even evidence to suggest that people who keep mentally active late in life by stimulating and challenging their intellectual abilities have a lower incidence of memory disorders including Alzheimer's disease.

Each time you learn something new, even a single new word, the qualities of the nerve cell endings change and nerve impulse transmission is enhanced.

You've heard it said that we only use a small fraction of our potential brainpower over the course of our lifetime. Be that as it may, there is clear evidence that brain function is remarkably changeable and that we possess enormous capacities for new learning. This is called *neuroplasticity*.

There are almost as many brain or mind exercises as there are physical or muscle building programs. Here are several common activities: studying languages; vocabulary building; mental games of every conceivable type; sculpture and/or painting. There are even several informal, everyday ways of exercising your mind. For example, the next time you are stuck in traffic or are at the checkout line of a supermarket,

- ◆ **Actively study the environment, deliberately focusing on the people, places, and objects that are within your vision.**
- ◆ **Enter a room and carefully notice the number of people, the clothes they are wearing, the placement of furniture and other objects.**
- ◆ **Write down everything you remember from an event you attend.**
- ◆ **Games — such as bridge, chess, checkers, crossword puzzles — will keep your brain active.**
- ◆ **For best results, move your body — that is exercise, stretch, take walks — as well as challenging your brain.**

Here's a final tip. Monotonous and repetitive work is not a good brain or mind exercise. Get some variety and stimulation.

❖   ❖   ❖

6. *Breaking Bad Habits*

❖

Constance found herself pulling her hair again. She had done so most of her life, but in the last few months became aware that her hair was actually thinning. She knew she had to stop. But how could she break a fifteen-year habit? Hugh wished he could stop biting his nails. "This annoying habit seems to have a firm grip on me!" he exclaimed. It was unlucky that he consulted a therapist who believed that it was necessary to explore Hugh's unconscious motives. This proved to be a waste of time and money.

❖

A lot of people develop simple but annoying habits that they find very hard to break: nail biting, hair pulling, skin picking, knuckle cracking, and a host of other disturbing behaviors.

Regardless of the nature of the habits, the technique of *habit reversal* usually works very well in breaking them. Constance and Hugh could have benefitted from habit reversal's five main components. Here's the first:

◆ **Recognize that the habit is a strong or persistent urge that is not rooted in deeper psychological problems.**

Unfortunately, there are still many mental health practitioners who maintain there is inevitably a deeper meaning behind simple habits and that it is necessary to unearth and treat this underlying process in order to break the habit successfully. Recent evidence shows this to be untrue.

The second step is to

◆ **keep precise records of urges and count the number of times that you actually succumb to them.**

It has been shown that the very process of counting and record keeping tends to give one an immediate sense of control over the habit.

The third element:

◆ **Develop an awareness of the chain of events that leads to or results in the unwanted behavior.**

For instance, you may find that boredom, watching TV, talking on the telephone, driving in the car, and doing routine tasks that call for very little concentration set off the habit you wish to break.

The next component:

◆ **Learn relaxation methods as a means of combating the urges.**

As soon as you become aware of the desire to give in to the habit, it is a good idea instead to sit down or lie down and start breathing slowly and rhythmically while deliberately letting go of tension throughout your body.

The final aspect of habit reversal:

- ◆ **Substitute a response that is incompatible with the unwanted behavior.**

For example, brushing your teeth instead of eating a cookie; petting your cat instead of twirling or pulling your hair; using your hands — gardening, drawing, typing, and so forth — instead of biting your nails or cracking your knuckles.

If you really desire to quit the habit, this five-easy-step process really works.

❖   ❖   ❖

7. Using an Emotional Thermometer

❖

Ronnie was inclined to fly off the handle. She was hypersensitive and tended to respond with exaggerated emotion to most situations. A close relative commented: "Just about everything about Ronnie adds up to an eleven on a ten point scale." Sometimes a deceptively simple method enables over-reactive people to respond appropriately.

❖

People tend to magnify situations, resulting in needless misery, anxiety and emotional upsets.

How do most of us go about disturbing ourselves? Mainly by making mountains out of molehills. Instead of recognizing that something is merely annoying, or irritating, or frustrating, and responding appropriately, we blow up the incident or event and feel dreadful.

Ronnie offers a typical example: When her in-laws came to dinner, her mother-in-law commented that the mashed potatoes were lumpy. Even if the lady were a carping critic, surely this put-down should not warrant more than a tinge of irritation in Ronnie. But instead, she made herself feel terribly hurt and insulted.

We recommend that you

♦ use an *"emotional thermometer,"* with a scale from zero to 100.

Zero means that everything is going well, there's no undue tension. 100 units denotes something truly life-threatening and catastrophic.

So how many points are warranted for the remark by Ronnie's mother-in-law? Surely no more than five to ten. But Ronnie seemed to give it a rating of ninety-five! Similarly, when her six-year-old son was given a detention for using curse words in class, Ronnie gave it a rating of fifty to seventy units. Had Ronnie been one of our patients, we'd have urged her to calibrate events so that she would stop over-reacting.

The process is quite simple but can be very effective:

♦ Whenever you feel upset, ask yourself to come up with a logical number on the emotional thermometer.

Ask yourself if the strength of your feeling is a ten, more than twenty or thirty, or maybe as high as sixty or seventy.

One of our clients said: "Whenever I am feeling angry or upset I have learned to ask myself if I am reacting or over-reacting. This helps me come up with a rational number which, in turn, changes my feelings because the number is usually less than I thought!"

Mislabeling is the problem. To call something *awful, dreadful,* or *terrible,* when it is merely rather troublesome, will cause you to over-react. "As you think, so shall you feel." So the next time you are upset over something,

♦ try to obtain an appropriate number on the emotional thermometer and see if you find yourself feeling less upset.

❖   ❖   ❖

8. A Special Empowering Image

❖

Leon had a demanding job and often felt stressed out. He grew concerned when his doctor told him that his blood pressure was too high. He discussed the situation with a close friend who mentioned a mental imagery method he had learned from a psychologist. At first, the process struck Leon as rather ridiculous, but he decided to give it a try. He found the result most satisfactory.

❖

People who can use their imaginations have a ready-made skill that can be put to good effect in many situations.

One very effective method is to

◆ **create a room of your own, in your imagination,**

a very special room exactly the way you want it to be in terms of size, layout, furnishings and colors.

This then becomes your own private and distinctive place, a sanctuary that you can visit any time you wish. When you need a refuge, when you need a place to recharge yourself, to lick your wounds, to get yourself together, to go and think, or for any other reason, you can quickly and easily go there.

The process is simple: get as comfortable as you can, relax, close your eyes, and allow your mind to create, in its own way and at its own pace, an image of a very special place. You can make your place extremely safe and private, a room of your very own, unknown to anyone but you, arranged any way you like. The best part: you can go there anytime you so desire.

Take your time... When you have a place in mind, try it out. Mentally walk around in it... Look out the window if it has one... Check out the feel, and smell and sounds of it... See if it's right for you, and remembering that the power of your mind is virtually unlimited, change whatever you want in order to make your special place exactly the way you want it.

In this imaginary room you can be totally yourself... You can get in touch with your inner resources... You can be aware of your strengths and positive feelings... You can determine what will be in your best interests... You can plan changes you want to make... You can do anything at all that you want to do at that moment.

◆ **Visit your special room often.**

The more you practice this, the quicker and easier it will be achieved. Even brief five-to-ten minute visits can be highly comforting or energizing ---- as you wish.

When you leave the room, you should feel alert, fully functioning, very refreshed, and ready to go about your business.

It has been said, "No matter where you go, there you are." By developing your own private imaginary sanctuary, no matter where you find yourself physically, you will have an emotionally safe place to go to.

❖   ❖   ❖

9. Using Paradoxical Techniques

❖

Clay was at his wit's end. His mother-in-law often offered him free and unwelcome advice in the form of personal attacks. He went toe-to-toe with her once or twice, but this only aggravated matters. "What can I do to get this woman off my back?" he asked. When Clay learned about paradoxical techniques, this soon put an end to his mother-in-law's forays.

❖

One of the greatest discoveries in psychology is the fact that

◆ **you can often correct or change behaviors, thoughts, or feelings for the better by trying to make them worse.**

Instead of responding *negatively* to destructiveness or irrationality ("Stop it, that's enough! We don't like it!"), *positive* responses are provided. ("That's marvelous, why don't you do more?").

The point is illustrated by the case of a five-year-old girl who incessantly sucked her thumb. Her parents were able to eliminate the habit by urging her to suck her thumb more and more, and by insisting that she not take it out of her mouth. Dr. Knight Dunlap was one of the first psychologists who reported curing individuals of a variety of undesirable habits (such as nail biting, tics and stuttering) by having them deliberately increase the habits. In professional lingo this is called "negative practice."

Also the famous psychiatrist Dr. Victor Frankl, began using a technique he called "paradoxical intention" (deliberately trying to do something you really want not to do), which helped people control a variety of problems.

Here's a simple clinical example. Liz, who was dating Marty, persistently inquired "Do you love me?" He reassured her and said so many times. But this did not stop her from repeatedly seeking his reassurance which was upsetting and irritating him. Finally, one day, when Liz asked (for the millionth time) "Do you love me?" Marty said: "No, I hate you. I only stick around to torture you."

"Reverse psychology," used appropriately, puts an end to the silly games and arbitrary tests that people impose on one another.

One of our colleagues is a true expert at using paradox. Recently, at a party, when he publicly espoused an unpopular point of view, someone turned to him and said, "You really are a stupid fool!" Instead of taking offense, he replied: "I know. I am colossally stupid. My level of stupidity is off the scale. What can I do about it?" The man who insulted him was speechless and everyone else laughed and found it funny.

What is the difference between "paradoxical communications" and "sarcasm"? Sarcasm is hostility disguised as humor. It is intended to hurt, and is often bitter and caustic. Paradoxical statements are usually in response to someone's unhelpful remarks or behaviors, and the intent is to unravel and clarify the issue by magnifying its absurdities. Sarcastic statements are expressed in a cutting manner; paradoxical remarks are delivered with humor.

❖   ❖   ❖

10. Enhancing Your Five Senses

❖

Stan was described by someone as "up in the stratosphere." He seemed to dwell on abstract intellectual issues to the exclusion of all else. He admitted that he did not particularly enjoy food, sex, music, or social gatherings, cutting himself off from most of the joys of living.

❖

Although Stan is an extreme case, we can all add more enjoyment and pleasure to our lives. How? By cultivating our senses! Too many of us are out of touch with our sensory delights, mainly because today's world is so packed with information that we are bombarded by visual and auditory cues ---- a barrage of sights, sounds and other sensory inputs that end up creating a kind of numbness.

Who has the time ---- or takes the time ---- these days, to fully relax and thoroughly enjoy the delights of a beautiful sunset, or a starry sky, a moving piece of music, an Epicurean meal, a good old-fashioned body rub, or the delightful aroma of a bouquet of flowers?

Most of our pleasures, most of the stimuli that make life worth living, are derived from our five senses ---- what we see, hear, touch, smell and taste.

- ◆ **The more you develop and attend to your senses, the greater the potential for enjoying life.**

It is significant that Albert Einstein's approach to learning emphasized using and integrating all of the senses. There are data to show that sense-stimulating activities tend to expand or enrich certain nerve cells in the brain.

There's a saying: "Try to please the eyeballs." In fact, more than half the body's sense receptors are clustered in the eyes.

- ◆ **Make a point of drinking in the delights of nature — the sky, the trees, the flowers, bodies of water, or whatever else you enjoy looking at.**
- ◆ **Try to sharpen all your senses.**

Seek out pleasant scents ---- the aroma of apple pie baking in the oven if you like that, the smell of fresh flowers, herbs and spices, or aromatic oils such as lavender, peppermint, rose, vanilla, orange, etc.

◆ **Listen to the music you love. The right melodies for you can soothe frayed nerves.**

And you can activate your sense of touch with these simple steps:

◆ **hug loved ones,**
◆ **pay attention to different textures,**
◆ **pet friendly animals,**
◆ **give or get a back rub,**
◆ **soak in a hot tub,**
◆ **take a relaxing shower.**

And don't just gulp your food.

◆ **Really make a point of tasting it.**

There is a vast array of physical and mental health benefits from tuning into and really paying attention to your senses.

❖   ❖   ❖

11. Problem Solving

❖

Eric tended to wallow in self-pity. "I have so many problems that I don't know what to do or where to start." Actually, Eric's list of problems was no greater than most people's — it was just that he had not tried to tackle any of them so they felt overwhelming. Eric was taught a five-step problem-solving sequence, learned how to be solution oriented, and matters started to change for the better.

Problems are inevitable. Some are simple or straight-forward, easily solved without much thought or planning. Other problems are complex or multifaceted and do not lend themselves to immediate or easy solutions.

Amazingly, despite all the schooling and education most of us go through, few people learn really effective strategies for problem solving, especially when it comes to common, everyday social or relationship issues.

Regardless of the nature or complexity of a problem, the following five-step method of rational problem solving almost always leads to workable solutions.

The first step in effective problem solving is to

◆ **define the problem as specifically and concretely as possible.**

"What exactly is bothering me?"

The second step is to

◆ **generate as many potential solutions as reasonably possible.**

Very importantly, this step simply involves generating a wide variety and quantity of possible solutions without evaluating them for merit or utility. The idea is that through quantity, a certain amount of quality will be produced. So, anything goes during this step — even what might appear to be ridiculous solutions.

The third step is to

◆ **evaluate the various solutions for merit and utility.**

This is done by conducting a straightforward pros and cons analysis of each possible solution. What are the respective advantages and disadvantages of each solution? Chances are that when this step is completed, one particular solution will be deemed the best among the group.

The fourth step is to

◆ **select the best solution and try it out.**

The fifth step is to

◆ **decide on the effectiveness of the implemented solution.**

If it worked, no more problem! If it failed to bring about an acceptable outcome, go back to step three and implement the second-best solution among those remaining.

If that doesn't do the trick, it might be a good idea to redo step two and generate additional potential solutions. If necessary, start the process over again by redefining the original problem.

❖   ❖   ❖

12. Meditation: Part 1

❖

*When Irwin was advised to learn how to use meditation to handle his
stress, he scoffed at the idea. "I've never felt comfortable in the lotus
position," he jeered. He also sneered that you have to be from India to
benefit from the technique. Too bad. Irwin's prejudices prevented him
from learning an important method that has literally helped millions.*

❖

Meditation involves various methods of mental and physical focusing that
often lead to a lowering of tension and anxiety and an increase in
contentment and tolerance of frustration. Most meditation techniques are
very old and are often connected with Eastern philosophy and the teachings
of various Indian gurus.

Perhaps the most widely known meditation method is "transcendental
meditation," or TM, which is usually associated with the Indian guru
Maharishi Mahesh Yogi. Maharishi began teaching the technique
throughout India in the 1950's, ultimately launching the world-wide TM
movement.

In the late 1960's and early 1970's, the TM movement swept across
the United States, and huge numbers of people flocked to TM teachers to
learn how to "unlock their hidden potentials" through the TM method.

Many advocates of TM made rather exaggerated claims about its
merits (suggesting it can raise IQs, eliminate the need for sleep, and cure
psychological problems) and needlessly surrounded it with secrecy and a
compelling mystique. Beyond the unwarranted hype, however, the fact
remains that TM and other related methods of meditation do have very
real mental and physical health-promoting effects.

Meditation appears to be a natural process, perhaps a "fourth state of
consciousness," quite distinct from waking, sleeping, or dreaming. Meditation
does not require any mental or physical control, any drastic changes in lifestyle
or belief system, nor does it involve hypnosis or suggestion.

In essence, meditation methods produce a hypometabolic state,
during which the activity of the autonomic nervous system is reduced. This
leads to a lower heart rate, reduced blood pressure, and more efficient
respiration which, in turn, produces a variety of positive psychological
effects, such as reduced levels of worry and anxiety and an increase in
emotional well-being.

❖   ❖   ❖

13. Meditation: Part 2

❖

Terry entered the office, presented himself to the secretary, and sat down to await his appointment with the boss. As he waited, he closed his eyes briefly, and he used the rapid meditation method he had learned. Even after less than half a minute he felt himself feeling calm and well-prepared for the meeting.

❖

So, how does one meditate? Basically, here's how it's done.

The first step is to

◆ **get into a comfortable and relaxing position.**

This can be sitting up, reclining, or lying down, as long as the position is comfortable for you.

Next,

◆ **breathe deeply and evenly.**

Instead of expanding your chest, let your abdomen rise when you inhale and fall when you exhale. Let the air flow in and out with as little effort as possible making sure not to breathe more deeply than you can comfortably manage.

You would then

◆ **think of a neutral or pleasant sounding word preferably with two syllables.**

Just about any word will do as long as it does not conjure up any negative or emotionally unsettling association. This is what is called the *mantra* and it's what one focuses on during meditation.

Let's use the word "relax" as our sample mantra. Once comfortable and breathing easily,

◆ **think or silently say to yourself the first syllable ("re") as you inhale.**
◆ **As you exhale, think the second syllable ("lax").**

The mantra is silently chanted during the entire inhalation-exhalation cycle.

While relaxing, and focusing on the rhythmic chanting of the mantra in cycle with your breathing,

◆ **let your thoughts and mental pictures float passively through the window of your consciousness.**

Don't push away or hold onto any particular thoughts or images no matter what they may be. Just let any and all thoughts come and go without any conscious interference and try to do this for about ten to twenty minutes without interruption.

- **If at any time you realize you've stopped chanting the mantra, just pick it up again.**

Think "reeee-laaaax, reeee-laaaax," in rhythm with your breathing.

Some people prefer to practice mini-meditations ---- three to five minutes ---- several times a day. You need to experiment to determine what suits you best.

❖   ❖   ❖

14. Rapid Relaxation Methods

❖

Carl used to be described as "uptight." In fact, he was such a taut person that he suffered from chronic back pain and excruciating headaches that his doctors ascribed to tension. He was also very anxious. When he learned to perform regular relaxation techniques, these problems came to an end. There are numerous studies to prove that for many people, the act of letting go of tense muscles, just performing simple relaxation maneuvers, has a most powerful and beneficial effect throughout the mind and body.

❖

If you are willing to devote about two minutes several times a day to simple relaxation methods, you might be amazed at the health-giving results.

Merely taking the weight off your feet, sitting down or lying down, letting tense muscles loosen up, and breathing more slowly, changes your blood chemistry and has a profound effect on your nervous system. If you made a point of doing this for about two minutes at a time, five to ten times a day, you would be decreasing your stress levels and producing several health-enhancing effects.

Please don't say that you are "too busy" to relax. All it takes is a total of ten to twenty minutes a day. When consulted by a very busy executive who suffered from many symptoms of stress, to begin with, we advised him to use these mini-relaxations throughout the day. He followed the advice and every now and then he would close his office door, take a couple of minutes to sit back, close his eyes, breathe deeply and slowly allow his muscles to go limp. He reported feeling more alert at work, better able to concentrate, and he would leave the office feeling less stressed out. This technique enabled him to derive many benefits from the remainder of his therapy.

Here's the simple process:

◆ **take a couple of minutes every few hours,**
◆ **sit back in a relaxed position,**
◆ **close your eyes,**
◆ **breathe slowly,**
◆ **let your tense muscles become loose,**
◆ **imagine a pleasant scene.**

Most of us work and stress ourselves without having a break from the tension. Many falsely believe that to derive benefit from relaxation, you must do it for twenty to thirty minutes at a time. Not true! Many people find themselves becoming more tense after prolonged relaxation.

Remember, all it takes is to sit down or lie down, let go of your muscles as best you can, and breathe slowly and deeply, for about two minutes. It is also often a good idea to conjure up positive images at the same time.

❖　❖　❖

15. Beating Insomnia

❖

Betty's poor sleep habits were getting her down. She took sleeping pills and tranquilizers from time to time, but hated to rely on pills — especially habit-forming drugs. She was not aware that some simple methods of "sleep hygiene" could be of enormous help to her.

❖

Almost everyone has occasional trouble sleeping. In fact, most people will have at least one bout of significant insomnia at some point during their lives.

While most episodes of insomnia are brief and self-limiting, in some cases insomnia is a sign of some underlying emotional, social, or even medical problem. If you suffer from persistent insomnia, a medical consultation is recommended.

Fortunately, the vast majority of insomnia sufferers can be helped simply by following seven guidelines of good sleep hygiene:

- ◆ **Avoid caffeine and alcohol, especially in the evening.**
- ◆ **Make sure to get plenty of regular exercise such as walking, but be careful not to overdo it.**
- ◆ **Use your bed only for sleep and sex — so avoid watching TV, eating, or even reading in bed.**
- ◆ **Unless they disagree with you, eat moderate amounts of foods rich in the sleep promoting amino acid tryptophan, such as poultry and milk.**
- ◆ **Try to keep the temperature of your bedroom on the cool side since excessive heat often interferes with deep, sound sleep.**
- ◆ **Stick to a consistent pattern of sleep time. Don't throw your body out of synch with erratic bed and wake times. So, as tempting as it might be to sleep in on weekends, don't do it if you're not sleeping well on week nights.**
- ◆ **And very importantly, don't force yourself to try to sleep.**

The last point is very important. If you can't fall asleep fairly quickly, get out of bed and do some non-strenuous activity, like reading in a comfortable chair, or playing a few rounds of solitaire, until you feel sleepy, then return to bed.

If these simple guidelines don't help within a few nights, consult your family doctor or a qualified mental health specialist.

❖   ❖   ❖

16. Beating Procrastination - Part 1

❖

Friday. 4:15 p.m. Glenn realizes the grant proposal has to be in the mail today or he stands no chance. The proposal is still in outline. Can he finish it, polish it, and mail it by 5:30? Tuesday. 6 p.m. Geneva will chair the PTA subcommittee on recreation programs in an hour. She hasn't looked at her notes since the last meeting, a month ago. As she gathers her materials, she realizes that she was to report estimates for the cost of referees for the after-school basketball program. She has made no effort to get the necessary information.

❖

Everyone occasionally puts off doing things, feels unmotivated, or avoids taking action. For most people the tendency to procrastinate is a basically normal attribute that, at worst, results in a little inconvenience or unnecessary time pressure.

Some people, however, seem to have enormous difficulty getting started and seem incapable of initiating tasks. Consequently these "expert procrastinators" frequently find themselves one or two steps in front of a virtual tidal wave of deadline stress, unfinished business, and loose ends.

Fortunately, regardless of whether you are a novice task avoider or a veteran activity delayer, there are several very powerful methods for beating procrastination and thereby increasing productivity while at the same time reducing stress.

The first and probably most important anti-procrastination method is simply to understand the relationship between motivation and action. Most people mistakenly believe that motivation must precede action ---- that before you can actually do something you must first feel motivated to do it. Right?

Wrong! The fact is that in most cases action precedes motivation ---- that is, once action has been initiated motivation tends to gather momentum and it becomes increasingly easy to continue what has been started. As the old saying goes: "Getting started is the hardest part."

♦ **Don't wait for motivation before taking action — make motivation by taking action!**

Many are deterred from starting a task or attending to a situation because it will only amount to a drop in the bucket. "So why bother?" they say, and simply proceed to do nothing. But one drop becomes two, then four, eight, sixteen, and fairly soon, significant headway has been made.

The next time you feel the creeping paralysis of procrastination taking hold of you, make a commitment to do just a few minutes of the task you are avoiding. You'll probably find that after the first few minutes elapse, the momentum of motivation will be solidly upon you and you'll continue the task with ever-increasing interest and enthusiasm.

❖   ❖   ❖

17. Beating Procrastination - Part 2

❖

Ken's friends kidded him about always putting things off. "If there were a Nobel Prize for procrastination," they said, "you'd be a sure winner." But the fact that Ken had been fired from three jobs in the past five months because of his delaying tactics was not at all funny.

❖

Another useful method for beating procrastination involves recognizing that the way you think will either stimulate and facilitate or deactivate and interfere with the process of getting started. Most procrastination-causing ideas can be called Task Interfering Thoughts or TITs. Alternatively, ideas that tend to motivate action can be called Task Activating Thoughts or TATs.

"I can cut the lawn tomorrow." "The report is not due until Friday." "I'll take out the recycling after I watch the news" are all examples of Task Interfering Thoughts or TITs. "If I cut the lawn now, I can relax the rest of the weekend," and "Better get started on that report in case something comes up between now and Friday," and "Let me take out the recycling right now so I can enjoy the rest of the evening without unfinished chores hanging over my head" are all examples of Task Activating Thoughts or TATs.

You've heard of the old saying "tit for tat"? Well, when it comes to beating procrastination, TAT for TIT is much more effective.

- ◆ Whenever you find yourself delaying or avoiding undertaking a chore, assignment, or job because of Task Interfering Thoughts — TITs — try to change them to Task Activating Thoughts — TATs — and see what a difference it makes.

It is also often useful to

- ◆ give yourself certain rewards after completing a task.

"If I finish this report on time, I will treat myself to a round of golf" (or some other reward that fits into your lifestyle). Remember,

- ◆ just getting started, no matter how far behind you may have fallen, will ignite the momentum of motivation.

By developing these anti-procrastination skills, you can become more productive while at the same time reducing stress.

THINKING YOURSELF HEALTHY

18. How You Think So Shall You Feel

❖

Gina complained that she felt down or upset a lot of the time. "I have no control over the way I feel," she said. When she learned that her thoughts were largely responsible for her feelings, she was able to gain much more control over her disturbing emotions. She found that, with a bit of effort and application, it became possible to control and alter many of her negative thoughts.

❖

Almost everyone has heard the saying "mind over matter." While it's doubtful that the human mind can control objects with pure mind power, what is becoming increasingly clear is that thoughts and perceptions can dramatically influence moods, feelings, and emotions.

How many times have you heard someone say, "That really made me mad," or "He upset me," or "It bothered me," as if external events had a direct control over our moods? The fact is

♦ **it's not events that trigger our emotions, rather it's how we think about events that determine our feelings.**

Our knee-jerk emotional reactions to external stimuli are really the combined effects of the external event and our *interpretation* of that event. That's the cognitive connection, the link that joins together events and emotions in the chain of our experiences.

This concept is at least two thousand years old and is often attributed to the philosopher Epictetus, who said "Men [and women] feel disturbed not by things, but by the views they take of them." Many centuries later, William Shakespeare rephrased this thought in *Hamlet* when he wrote: "There (is) nothing either good or bad but thinking makes it so."

The fact is, we have tremendous control over our emotions and are not helpless stimulus-response creatures who are powerless over our moods.

♦ **Simply recognizing that thinking influences emotions is a very important step on the road leading to a happier and healthier life.**

Negative thoughts can be challenged and changed. This, in turn, leads to more positive feelings and emotions.

❖   ❖   ❖

19. How to Be Happier by Thinking Healthier

❖

"I'm actually very pleased that Joe broke off our relationship." None of Elaine's friends believed her. It was evident to them that she was really very hurt and puzzled by Joe's behavior. By rationalizing, instead of facing the truth, Elaine was preventing herself from learning how to stop repeating the same mistakes.

❖

In the previous segment, we pointed out that thinking is a critically important link in the chain of events that joins together external situations and our emotional responses to them. Remember, events don't make us mad, sad, glad, or scared; rather it's our *interpretations* of the events that lead us to feel mad, sad, glad, or scared.

There are three basic ways of thinking. We can think rationally, irrationally, or we can rationalize. *Rational thinking* is based more on objective fact than subjective opinion. It assists us in survival, helps us in achieving goals, and promotes emotional well-being and relationship success.

Irrational thinking is not based on reason or objectivity ⸺ it tends to undermine emotional well-being, often leads to unnecessary conflict, and at times even threatens survival.

Rationalization is basically a con job ⸺ an attempt to explain away actions or choices with seemingly valid, but actually bogus, justifications.

Although not as unhealthy as pure irrationality, rationalization is no friend of mental health either.

◆ **Clearly, the healthiest type of thinking is rational thinking.**

Unlike irrational beliefs that are almost always based on demanding shoulds and musts, or what are called "categorical imperatives," rational thought is based on preferences, acceptance, and tolerance.

The bottom line is simple. If you want to make yourself happier and promote better relationships,

◆ **try to eliminate the shoulds and musts from your thoughts**

and replace them with more balanced rational self-talk. Instead of saying, "I must do X and I must have Y," say, and really mean, "I'd very much prefer doing X and having Y, but I don't absolutely have to do or get anything."

Please keep in mind that rational thinking doesn't mean unemotional living! On the contrary.

◆ **Replacing irrational beliefs with rational ones simply reduces negative emotions and simultaneously increases positive feelings.**

❖ ❖ ❖

20. The Tyranny of the Should

❖

Al could not understand why he had no close friends. He saw himself as honest and caring. What he did not realize was that he had so many shoulds, oughts and musts that it was impossible to be around him without being corrected or criticized. "One thing I don't need," said an acquaintance, "is endless free advice."

❖

People who use too many shoulds, oughts, musts and have-tos are very demanding and unpleasant, and they make life miserable for themselves and others. We see many people in our consulting rooms who make demands, who strongly insist on things. They typically have a history of acrimonious divorce, no friends, and many problems on the job.

Known as "categorical imperatives," shoulds, oughts and musts create anger and guilt. "You *should* have done X and not Y!" "He *should* have known better!" are expressions of anger. "I *shouldn't* have said that!" "I *should* have done XYZ!" are statements of guilt.

When people are able to drop their demands, to change their shoulds into preferences, amazing benefits often result.

♦ **Try to catch yourself each time you lay a should, ought or must on someone.**

Change the should into a request or a preference. Instead of angrily saying, "You *should* have introduced me to your cousin!" you can say, "I *wish* you had introduced me to your cousin." Instead of insisting, "You *must* not smoke in the house!" you can say, "I'd *prefer* that you smoke outside."

♦ **Change should, ought, must into "I wish" or "I'd prefer" and see what happens.**

We predict that the fewer shoulds, oughts and musts you use, the better off you, your loved ones and your associates will be.

It's obviously not just the word "should" that creates the problem, it's the demanding should. There's nothing wrong with saying "You should remember to take the recycling bins to the curb if you want them to be collected." That's what we call a "soft should." It differs from the demanding should, in that soft shoulds have an "if" statement following them that mentions a specific consequence. "You should have known better than to leave the dishes in the sink!" Compare that to: "You should put your dish in the dishwasher if you want to help me clean up." Better yet, try to state the request without using the word "should" at all, such as, "Please try to remember to put your dishes in the dishwasher."

❖   ❖   ❖

21. More about Shoulds and Musts

❖

*Norman, a twice-divorced thirty-six-year-old lawyer, came for therapy.
He often ran into interpersonal problems, but recently he had lost three
close friendships, had a serious falling out with his parents, and his fiancée
had broken off their engagement. No wonder! Norman had more rules
and regulations than the Army, Navy and Air Force combined.*

❖

The enslaving power of personal rules was first recognized by the
world-renowned psychiatrist Dr. Karen Horney, who wrote about "the tyranny
of the should," a theme later expanded by Dr. Albert Ellis, President of the
Albert Ellis Institute in New York City, who coined the terms "shoulding"
and "musturbating" to emphasize the psychologically destructive power of
categorical imperatives like shoulds and musts. Dr. Ellis advises that

- **people stop "shoulding" on others and themselves, and avoid
  "musturbating" as much as possible.**

Norman's excessive shoulds and musts led him to break off contact
with his brother for making investments that Norman regarded as
ill-advised, and he was irate about a whole slew of things. His life changed
for the better when he managed to exorcise his shoulds.

At the end of his therapy, Norman wrote the following note, which
we encourage you to adopt for your own life:

- **"I have decided to abrogate responsibility for other people's lives.
  I let others decide what should and shouldn't apply to them."**

Norman continued: "This has lifted an enormous burden from my
shoulders. I don't take life as seriously as I did, and I let God decide what
should and shouldn't be. All I know is what I like, what I dislike and what
I wish for." Six months later, on a follow-up questionnaire, he wrote: "For
the first time in my life I believe that I would be called 'popular.' I don't
know how anybody put up with me before."

Unlike Norman, many people are unwilling or unable to drop their
shoulds and musts. "You should have known better!" "You must stop doing
that!" "I should have behaved differently." "I must win the tennis game!"

- **Catch your own shoulds and musts, change them into
  preferences or wishes:**

"I'd like to win the tennis game." "I wish you'd stop doing that." Try out
this technique and see how much better you feel.

❖   ❖   ❖

22. The Dangers of Faulty Positive Thinking

❖

Isaac suffered from what could be called "blinding optimism." He focused exclusively on the bright side of life, on all the good events. By sweeping harsh realities under the rug, he was often taken by surprise when unmistakably negative circumstances arose. He was often off guard and unprepared due to his ever-present rose-colored glasses.

❖

Most Americans are familiar with Norman Vincent Peale and his writings on "the power of positive thinking." Basically, this sounds like excellent advice. And indeed, Dr. Martin Seligman, a top-notch research psychologist and a President of the American Psychological Association, has shown that "optimism" is a key element in emotional well-being.

But there is a big difference between healthy optimism and the Pollyanna pop psychology version of positive thinking. Giddy positivism advises us to look on the bright side at all times. These trite pep talks often tend to backfire and cause resentment and isolation in others.

People who play the "everything-will-be-terrific" game not only overlook real problems and issues that need to be addressed, but they prevent others from expressing grief, pain, anger, loneliness, or fears. It is difficult if not impossible to air your true feelings in the presence of one of these ever-positive thinkers. They often make others feel guilty for harboring bad feelings.

◆ **Realistic optimists do not talk about how wonderful things are, how terrific everything will turn out, when faced with genuinely bad or unfortunate events.**

Those who believe if you smile in the face of tragedies, if you keep on chanting that everything will turn out wonderfully, often end up with even bigger problems.

◆ **Small problems, when ignored, glossed over or denied, have a way of spreading and growing into big problems.**

The difference between false optimism and rational optimism can be captured by two different statements. (1) "There's nothing to be concerned about, everything will be just grand." That's false optimism. The second statement reflects realistic optimism: (2) "We've got a real mess on our hands, things don't look too good, but if we tackle it step by step, we can probably do something about it."

It is also important to realize that

- **in some circumstances change cannot be achieved, and it is acceptance, not optimism, that will prevent depression or endless frustration.**

❖ ❖ ❖

23. Nobody's Perfect!

❖

Harry wanted the perfect wife, the perfect job, and the perfect home. At age thirty-nine he was still unmarried, unemployed, and living in a tenement. His quest for perfection had made it virtually impossible for Harry to be satisfied with the offerings of the real world.

❖

Perfectionists are unrealistic. Few things and no people are perfect. To expect perfection from yourself or from others only creates an impossible standard and can result in a downward spiral of negative thinking that leads to self-criticism, dissatisfaction, frustration, resentment and a "why bother" attitude.

At a recent social gathering, one of the guests proudly stated: "I'm a perfectionist!" He was rather taken aback when we said: "We're sorry to hear it. You have our sympathy."

- **If you push yourself to perform perfectly, you may find that your efforts are counter-productive.**

Forcing yourself to meet unrealistic expectations invites undue stress, anxiety, and burnout. In fact, perfectionism often encourages unhealthy competition and may even promote unethical behavior (cheating on exams, taking credit for others' work or falsely claiming job qualifications).

- **Learn to give yourself permission not to perform at optimum speed every minute of the day.**

Instead, strive to be competent, to perform extremely well at times but not perfectly, to realize that there are days when you feel under the weather, you are preoccupied with a personal problem, or you feel that the task at hand just does not seem that important. Freed from the pressure to perform perfectly, you will enjoy the work much more, and the result will be good, often excellent work.

◆ **It's most important to accept the fact that some things only need to be "good enough."**

It's also important to realize that if you aim too high, you will miss the mark. Wise people learn to derive enjoyment from a task instead of dwelling on the outcome.

If you fail to achieve a perfect (impossible) standard or goal, you are not a failure. The failure is due to the fact that the goal was impossible in the first place.

❖   ❖   ❖

24. Unhappiness Is Self-Created

❖

Caroline was not a happy woman. She saw herself as a victim of circumstances. She blamed her unhappiness on a long list of external factors (other people, the economy, the weather, the government, her employer...), never dreaming that her own perceptions were primarily behind her miserable feelings.

❖

The widespread tendency to attribute unhappiness to external sources is one of the most serious psychological mistakes. People say: "His remark upset me!" "Her comments hurt me!" "It made me unhappy when he snubbed me!"

In reality, it is not remarks, comments and statements that cause hurt or upset. People *upset themselves* over these statements or incidents. The age-old saying (like most age-old sayings) remains profoundly true: "Sticks and stones may break my bones but words can never hurt me!"

Though we utter these ideas as children, we do not take them seriously as adults. If we did, we would then say, correctly, "I upset myself over his remark," in place of the psychologically inaccurate version, "His remark upset me!" We would say: "I hurt myself over her comments," "I made myself unhappy when he snubbed me."

◆ **As long as we incorrectly blame outside sources for our miseries, we cannot do much about them. However, if we realize that we upset ourselves over the things that happen to us, we can work at changing.**

For example, a young man was extremely distressed because his girlfriend refused to stop dating other men. "Her behavior really upsets me," he said. "No," we replied, "you are upsetting yourself over her behavior." And then we asked: "How are you managing to upset yourself so deeply?"

It didn't take long to piece together the fact that he was upsetting himself by engaging in a whole series of faulty ideas, or irrational self-talk. We were then able to show him how to stop making himself so unhappy over his girlfriend's lack of ardor.

◆ **By recognizing that the way you think about events determines how you feel, you'll be able to take control instead of being controlled.**

If you make yourself unhappy when your in-laws visit you, or when someone puts you down, first discover how you go about inducing this unhappiness. What are you telling yourself? Then you can decide to do something about it. You can disarm faulty reasoning and find yourself indifferent instead of making yourself miserable.

❖   ❖   ❖

25. Beware of High Expectations

❖

Brad worked as a factory supervisor. He expected his employees to start work on time, to avoid dallying around the coffee pot, and to observe the proper lunch breaks. He cut his workers little slack. He was not a perfectionist but his excessive expectations landed him in hot water. Those who worked for him saw Brad as a source of stress and they presented upper management with a signed petition asking that he be replaced.

❖

Note the difference between *perfectionism*, which is also an unfortunate trait, and *excessive expectations*. If Brad were a perfectionist, he would have insisted that his workers turn out perfect products. This was not his problem. His high expectations were not tied to achievement or performance but centered on clock-watching demands, and his rigid sense of productive time vs. wasted time.

Here are some other examples: When Don told Celia exactly what he expected from a wife, his expectations struck her as so demanding and petty that she broke off the engagement there and then --- and had a lucky escape. Janice expected her husband to remember her birthday and their wedding anniversary, as well as the birthdays and anniversaries of her three sisters. Tom expected other people always to be punctual, and he became irate when they kept him waiting. Sally was deeply hurt when her son and daughter-in-law did not invite her for Christmas; she had expected to be invited.

- **The fewer expectations you have, the less upset and disappointed you will be.**

One wise individual remarked: "I try not to expect anything from anyone. That way, I rarely feel hurt, upset, let down, disillusioned, or disappointed. I have also learned not to expect too much from myself."

- **The key question to ask yourself is whether you are being unreasonable in your desires and expectations.**

If there is any doubt in your mind, ask a close friend to give you an objective opinion.

Unreasonable expectations lead to disappointment, letdowns and unhappiness. Reasonable expectations set the stage for success, satisfaction and optimum performance.

❖   ❖   ❖

26. On Making Judgements vs. Being Judgemental

❖

Howard was nicknamed "the judge." He hadn't spoken to his older brother for three years as a result a minor incident. One of his coworkers said, "He brings to mind a kangaroo court in which the judge eagerly slams down the gavel and shouts 'Guilty!' And that's why he's excluded from all the social activities in the office."

❖

Judgemental, prejudiced and biased individuals make far-reaching pronouncements based on limited information. We all know such people. Their false and extreme generalizations give them away. "Anyone who uses curse words is obviously stupid and uneducated!" "Rock-and-roll fans don't know the first thing about music!" "People who don't regularly attend religious services are heathens!"

Most people realize that being judgemental is an unattractive trait. If you look around, you'll find that most judgemental people are disliked and avoided. The answer to Mom's reproach, "Why don't you call your mother more often?" if truthful would probably be, "Because you're judgemental and tend to pick on me, so it's unpleasant to talk to you." When people stop being judgemental, they often discover a level of personal happiness that had eluded them.

Yet none of us can help forming opinions of other people. So how does judgemental thinking differ from making judgements? Judgemental people state their views and observations in authoritative terms; they decree what is right and wrong, what should and should not be, what is good or bad. Making a simple judgement, however does not carry these ominous overtones. "Billy has poor table manners" is a judgement. The judgemental person would add something, such as "Therefore, he's a slob who was raised by cavemen!"

We make judgements constantly. "He's good-looking." "She dresses well." "He seems to lack a good sense of humor." "She's overweight."

◆ **In forming opinions or making judgements, there is no moral overtone, no further conclusions are drawn, no inferences are made about the person's character, we just have the observation or the perception.**

As soon as we add "therefore" to the observation, we are likely to be judgemental. "He talks very slowly," is an observation, "therefore, he must be stupid" is a judgemental conclusion.

- ◆ **If you look out for your own "therefores" you are less likely to sit in judgement over your fellow human beings, which will be all to the good for you and for them.**

❖ ❖ ❖

27. Jumping to Conclusions

❖

Charles met Debbie at a friend's wedding and found her to be very attractive. A few weeks later, he invited her to join him for dinner with two other couples. Debbie was so quiet throughout the evening that Charles lost interest in her then and there. "She's a total bore!" he said. A mutual friend who knew Debbie very well assured Charles that Debbie was usually vivacious and lots of fun. "Maybe Debbie had one of her low-grade migraine headaches," Charles's friend explained, "and that's why she was so withdrawn and quiet." Charles didn't buy it. He insisted that Debbie was a "non-person."

❖

Have you noticed how many people jump to conclusions; how they form opinions about people and events on extremely limited exposure? Do you tend to go by first impressions?

Those who arrive at premature conclusions, who don't obtain sufficient information to draw well-reasoned conclusions, are likely to be wrong and will suffer accordingly.

- ◆ **Whenever you make generalizations or draw conclusions based on limited exposure, you are likely to be wrong.**

After a brief visit to England, John decided that he'd like to live there and was delighted to accept a job offer. Within a week he realized that he'd made a serious mistake. Had he examined the situation and lifestyle more carefully, he'd have realized that he'd need to change too drastically to fit in. Meanwhile, he lost his well-paying job in this country and created a major problem for himself.

It will be greatly to your benefit to dig for facts rather than jump to conclusions.

- **Ask yourself if you have asked enough questions to check out your assumptions.**

Asking whether there are aspects or elements about which you're unaware could be helpful. Ask: "Do I really know the whole story?"

- **Aim for balance. Look before you leap (but don't keep on looking so hard and so long that you end up missing the boat!).**

❖   ❖   ❖

28. Avoiding Self-Fascism

Zelda was very intolerant of herself. She was kind and merciful towards others, but the standards she set for herself were severe. She was so hard on herself that she frequently punished herself psychologically ⁓ or even denied herself everyday comforts ⁓ if she fell short of her ideals.

❖

Fascist governments are autocratic, dictatorial and prone to force and brutality. Severe criticisms and cruel condemnations, even for minor infractions, are typical fascistic reactions. When witnessing people treating someone in that harsh manner, most of us feel repelled and disgusted.

But it is not only governments who may be guilty of such inhumane treatment. Have you ever been at a social gathering where one person verbally attacked another? "You stupid fool!" "You selfish pig!" "You ungrateful creep!" Such statements are common put-downs that we term *fascistic*. They are extremely unpleasant to witness, and the attacker loses respect within moments.

Most people would say: "I'd never speak to anybody like that. I know better than to assault someone's dignity and self-esteem." However,

- **many people who would not dream of talking to anybody else in a fascistic manner, often do so to themselves.**

They say things like: "I'm such an idiot! I'm a real jerk! I'm a stupid moron!" Although they would never address someone else like that, they think it is perfectly fine to treat themselves that way. Well, it isn't fine at all.

It makes no difference if someone sees you putting yourself down or if they observe you putting someone else down. To them you are another person, and whether such unkindness emanates from someone else or comes from yourself, they are still witnessing another person being subjected to abuse.

Fascism is equally despicable whether you treat others like a dictator or direct tyrannical invectives at yourself.

◆ **It pays huge psychological dividends to talk to and about yourself with the same respect that you normally pay to others.**

❖ ❖ ❖

29. Mistakes Can Be Beautiful

Gary was amazed when one of the men at the office openly admitted having made some mistakes that morning. "I wonder why he didn't cover it up?" Gary thought to himself. He had been raised to believe that making mistakes is an indication of inferiority. Gary went out of his way to avoid making any blunders whatsoever.

❖

Many people will find the following statement completely puzzling: "To make mistakes can be beautiful, not simply tolerable, not merely acceptable, not only necessary, but actually desirable."

"That doesn't make any sense!" we hear you exclaiming. "People think less of me if I make mistakes. Making mistakes is a sign of weakness. Anyone who makes a mistake appears stupid or foolish!"

Because so many people believe those unfortunate ideas, if they make a mistake they deny it, or try to cover it up. In truth,

◆ **one of the major ways of learning is through correcting mistakes. Mistakes provide clues for further growth.**

Assuming you must be "right all the time" is strongly anti-growth and leads to the constant need to be on guard and to cover up. It leaves you tense and defensive.

- ◆ **Most people who observe mistakes will probably be relieved to see that you are human, and closer relationships will be possible.**

Much unhappiness comes from the widespread and regrettable notion that it is important to avoid making mistakes in most situations, at all costs.

Harold was a junior business executive with many creative ideas, but he was too afraid to stick his neck out and mention them in case he might be wrong and thus not be promoted. When he received his evaluation, his boss regarded Harold as unimaginative and therefore he was not promoted.

There are no absolute rules in this area, of course. In certain situations it is advisable to cover up mistakes, but such situations are few and far between. In fact, many good therapists tell their clients to draw attention to some mistakes instead of covering them up. We've often said: "Tell your friends about some of your major mistakes." Those who follow this advice say that

- ◆ **admitting errors gets easier and even enjoyable with practice.**

You might even deliberately go out of your way to make some minor mistakes that are sure not to hurt anyone else. Allowing yourself to be genuinely human can be a valuable lesson in humility and stress management!

❖   ❖   ❖

30. On Facts and Opinions

❖

Henry was regarded as opinionated. "I just saw the best movie of the decade," he announced to some associates. Chris said, "You mean you have just seen a movie that you enjoyed." "No," said Henry, "I know the difference between a good and a bad motion picture." Gordon chimed in. "Most of the time," he said, "it seems to be a matter of opinion." "Wrong!" Henry exclaimed, "it is a matter of fact."

❖

Do you know anyone who speaks with great certainty about everything, someone who makes statements such as, "Utter nonsense!" or "That's ridiculous!" or "You're completely wrong!" when someone disagrees with him or her?

Such people are often insufferable and are seldom popular. Their philosophy is "I *think* I know, therefore I *do* know!" Or they declare, "My opinion is not just an opinion, but a fact."

Being right is very important to such people, even when they are dead wrong. They fail to realize that there is a big difference between *fact* and *truth* on the one hand, and *opinion, belief, taste,* and *preference* on the other. What's more, what is *wrong* is not the same as what we *dislike* or *disapprove of.*

A fact can be tested or checked: Lincoln was born in 1809; that cereal contains a lot of sugar. A belief, opinion, taste or preference cannot: corn tastes better than peas; long hair is more attractive than short hair.

Every person has a right to express opinions without being ridiculed or shouted down. It's important to avoid attacking or labeling those who disagree with us.

◆ **When not dealing with clear-cut facts, practice saying "It seems to me... It's my impression... I think... I believe... It's my opinion...."**

Be on guard against people who say, in effect "You are wrong... I am right... You have no taste... You have no brains... You don't know what's good...."

If someone says to you "You have no taste" you can politely but assertively correct the person by saying "You mean your taste differs from my taste." You are entitled to say "This may be a great painting but I don't particularly like it!"

But if you say "This is a rotten, lousy painting" you'd better be a recognized art connoisseur who is able to explain exactly why, in your opinion, that piece of art falls short.

❖ ❖ ❖

31. Setting Realistic Goals

❖

Derek lived by the adage, "reach for the stars." He believed that any position except at the very top was worthless. He did not realize that some of his lofty aspirations were beyond his true capabilities, and he was often disappointed and unhappy.

❖

Many people say: "If you want to attain a goal, go for it! Just do it!" And when people fail to achieve what they set out to do, they are often told, "You're just not trying hard enough." This criticism is often incorrect, and sometimes quite toxic.

For example, one of our clients, let's call him Bob, felt like a failure because, try as he might, he was never able to build a muscular physique or develop into a good athlete. His father and two brothers were all very athletic and well-built. Bob admired them greatly and wanted to emulate them, but unfortunately, he had not inherited their physical characteristics and natural athletic abilities. Instead of deluding himself about being capable of becoming an athlete, Bob needed to stop trying to be like his father and brothers and to pursue goals that lay within his grasp.

Another client, Sean, steered clear of the gym and the sporting field (despite the fact that his father was a physical education teacher). Instead, he became a tournament chess and bridge player.

- ◆ **It is important to strike a balance between perseverance and knowing when to quit.**
- ◆ **You need to assess your interests, abilities and goals and take an honest self-inventory.**

If a goal lies within your reach, by all means go for it. But if the strain is too much, you need to reassess the situation.

Don't try to split a granite rock by banging your head on it! Or, to use a different metaphor, remember to shift gears.

- **If your plans are not working out and you are feeling tired, discouraged and frustrated, try something else.**

A "switcher" is not the same as a quitter. A quitter does not give something a proper try but throws in the towel prematurely, just as soon as the going gets tough. But, if you give something a real effort and are still unsuccessful,

- **taking a different direction can remove your frustration, and you'll grow as a result.**

❖   ❖   ❖

32. Sticks and Stones May Break My Bones

Susan was extremely sensitive. A real or imagined slight, a harsh glance, an overlooked letter, a minor criticism would send her into the depths of gloom and anguish. Her sister remarked: "Susan gets hit by emotional Mack trucks ten times a day!"

❖

We'd like to reemphasize a theme that runs through many of the strategies in this book because it is so fundamental. In fact, we all learned to say it as children: "Sticks and stones may break my bones but words can never hurt me!"

Unfortunately, although most of us uttered these words when other kids were taunting us, we did not really believe them. The saying was merely a convenient way of appearing to be indifferent. Inside, the hurt and anger remained. It's probably impossible for a child to realize the basic truth ⸺ that words cannot hurt us but that we hurt ourselves over those words.

Try to convince a seven-, eight-, nine- or ten-year-old child that he does not have to get upset over the fact that some kids were teasing him about his orthodontic braces by calling him "buck teeth" or "metal mouth!" Try to persuade a twelve-year-old girl that she does not need to upset herself when her underdeveloped peers taunt her about wearing a bra.

Children ⸺ or adults ⸺ may say "words can never hurt me," but they do allow themselves to be hurt by name-calling, ridicule, teasing, and insults.

Bright, ten-year-old Andrew was upset because two boys had called him a "nerd." We had no success convincing him that they were probably just jealous of his high intelligence and the fact that he always got good grades.

Most people seem to have a desperate need to be liked, to be popular, and to be seen as "cool." They carry these desires with them throughout life ⸺ they earnestly seek approval, want to be liked (sometimes at all costs), and are often devastated by criticism and rejection.

What are the chances of enabling adults to fully realize that they don't have to upset themselves over other people's words?

- **If someone is putting you down, it is the speaker, the critic, who probably has emotional problems. Well-balanced individuals do not put others down.**

Any person who fully grasps this essential piece of wisdom will have the power to ignore negative criticism and emerge unscathed.

Look at it this way: If you visited a psychiatric hospital, and one of the severely disturbed patients in the locked unit criticized you viciously, you wouldn't take it to heart. You would consider the source of the put-down and ignore it. Just because another person who hurls insults at you is not a psychiatric patient, there's still no reason to take this person's criticisms to heart.

- **Other people, and the words they utter, have only as much power as you give them.**

❖   ❖   ❖

33. Three Basic Demands Typical of Neurotic People

❖

Bonnie grew up expecting life to be simple and easy for her. She came from a wealthy family, attended a small private school, and never had to contend with very much adversity, or even to take care of herself. When she entered college and left her over-protective environment where everyone had pampered her, she fell apart. Now she was expected to make it on her own, to be independent, but Bonnie had no skills — or desire — to face life alone.

❖

Imagine going through life with these three demands: "I must do well," "Others must treat me well," and, "I should never have to deal with hardships or difficulties." Some people actually believe that they should never be caught in a traffic jam, have to wait their turn in line, deal with red tape, or suffer any of life's small indignities.

The antidote is to abandon all demands. As Dr. Albert Ellis put it, "I now almost always think that it would be better or nicer if I did well, others treated me fairly, and the world proved easy and pleasant. But it doesn't have to turn out those ways — and that makes quite a difference!"

Dr. Ellis is one of the most acclaimed, prolific and widely cited authors in the field of clinical psychology. The innovator of a treatment he calls Rational Emotive Behavior Therapy, Ellis has identified three demands that underlie neurotic functioning.

The first demand — "I must do well" — is referred to as an "ego mandate." Simply stated, this means that:

♦ **people often place unduly high expectations on themselves.**

They insist that they must always live up to their ideals. "I must do well. I must be successful. I must be competent. I must achieve whatever I am capable of accomplishing. If I do not attain these goals, if I fail to live up to my expectations, I am a miserable failure and deserve the worst." This kind of thinking is the basis of self-denigration, self-hatred, self-downing and self-abnegation.

The second demand — "Others must treat me well" — shows itself when:

♦ **people hold the unreasonable expectation that others must treat them respectfully, fairly, considerately and decently.**

When this fails to occur, or when others are less than kind, courteous and respectful, the person's rage becomes extreme and the basic sentiment is that the perpetrators deserve nothing but the worst. Such attitudes are behind hatred, anger, hostility and rage.

The third neurotic demand is that "I should never have to deal with hardships or difficulties."

- ◆ **People drive themselves crazy believing that other people, circumstances, or the world at large should not disappoint or inconvenience them.**

They insist that mother earth should provide them with what they want quickly and easily. Such individuals suffer from low frustration tolerance and tend to magnify any setbacks into major catastrophes.

You can easily see how unrealistic and self-defeating these demands are. It takes hard and diligent work to let go of them, but the results fully justify the efforts.

❖ ❖ ❖

GETTING YOUR ACT(IONS) TOGETHER

34. Actions Speak Louder than Words

❖

Barbara and Jeff had a turbulent marriage, mainly because Jeff often disregarded Barbara's wishes and feelings. He would declare his undying love for her, but the way he behaved seemed to belie his words. He failed to call her when he was late, often overlooked birthdays and anniversaries, and made important family decisions without consulting her.

❖

Many people mistakenly believe that what we think, imagine or feel is as important as what we do. The truth is that, as the old familiar saying goes, "actions speak louder than words." Deeds truly are more important than thoughts.

While we may empathize with other people, we can never really know another person's thoughts, motivations, imagination, or emotional experiences. All we have to go by when forming opinions or making judgements about other people is the track record of their behavior, what they do or don't do.

Likewise, you know your own inner thoughts, feelings and motives, but the only information other people have to go on when forming opinions about you is your behavior. And what you choose to do, or decide against doing, is almost entirely within your voluntary control.

When taking a personal inventory, try not to overemphasize the importance of thoughts, feelings or motives at the expense of actions, deeds, or behaviors.

◆ **Remember our actions define us as individuals; people can't read your mind but they can see what you do.**

Still, many people needlessly "beat themselves up" emotionally because they believe their motives weren't pure or benevolent even though what they did was helpful or kind. But the truth is that even if you have uncharitable thoughts while doing charitable deeds, the deeds are nevertheless good!

Ultimately, what we do and don't do steers the course of our present lives and future experiences. What we do or don't do matters much more than what we think, feel, or imagine. To repeat:

- **What you think matters less than what you do.**
- **What is important is how you act.**

Remember that the thought is not equivalent to the act. Someone who thinks evil thoughts but only performs good deeds is still a good person.

❖   ❖   ❖

35. Learn to Delegate: Don't Do Everything Yourself

❖

Jack and Kent are next door neighbors who decided to add decks to their homes. Jack spent almost the entire summer building the deck himself while Kent hired a contractor and spent most of his time at the shore. There would be no problem if do-it-yourselfer Jack and his family had enjoyed the effort he expended. But he found the project to be tedious and exhausting, and his wife and children resented the fact that he spent hardly any time with them. Jack speaks of the project proudly, but he and his family paid a steep price for his pride.

❖

How many times have you heard someone say: "If you want something done right, do it yourself!" The do-it-yourself tradition runs deep in the American psyche. Visions of pioneers cutting logs and building cabins in the wilderness haunt our lumber yards and hardware stores on Saturday mornings.

Actually, oftentimes if you want to get something done (or done well) your best bet *is* to do it yourself. But like any "often truth" this attitude can be carried too far. There are many people who want to be in control, who have big ego investments in saying "I did it myself," and simply don't trust anyone else to handle a job well. Because they have trouble delegating responsibility to others, backlogs jam up their lives.

- ◆ **Ask for help, delegate responsibility to others, and utilize the talents of professionals. You'll be freer to attend to more important matters, and you'll enhance the quality of your life.**

A mechanical engineer complained that whenever he hired workers around the house, the jobs they did were not as good as he could have done himself. But in therapy, he learned to settle for something "good enough" rather than "perfect" and he became generally more relaxed and much less anxious.

A friend of ours with a sense of humor said: "Never do anything yourself that you can leave to others."

We say:

- ◆ **Set priorities, balance your responsibilities, do what you enjoy and can do, and delegate more often.**

❖   ❖   ❖

36. About Working Productively

❖

Gerry and Lionel were in the same graduate study group. Lionel put in at an extra five or six hours of study a day, while Gerry spent much of his free time relaxing. In terms of intelligence, nobody would dispute the fact that Lionel was smarter, but in the end, Gerry received an "A," Lionel a "B." When it came to the exam, could it be that Lionel had overdone it and burned out, while Gerry remained fresh and alert?

❖

Everyone knows that hard and diligent work often pays off, but many believe that the harder one works the more he or she will achieve.

We are told: "Keep your nose to the grindstone!" Frankly, we've never believed this expression --- unless someone wanted to whittle down or saw off his or her nose.

Of course, behind this awkward metaphor lies the notion that one should not goof off. But psychological studies show that

◆ **a certain degree of goofing off is good for you and will make you
more, not less, productive.**

Studies conducted on what is called "massed practice" versus
"distributed practice" almost always show that people who use massed
practice accomplish less than those who use distributed practice.

Massed practice means sticking to a task without taking a break or
having a rest, virtually working around the clock. Such hard workers usually
find that after a while, fatigue by-products build up in their bodies so that
they have to exert more and more effort to achieve worthwhile results.

Distributed practice refers to the strategy of taking short but fairly
frequent breaks. You stop what you are doing and take a ten-minute walk,
or call a friend, or do some relaxation exercises, or carry out some other
activity that differs from the task you are working at. Those who use
distributed practice are able to break the monotony, replenish their energy
levels and keep working at a faster and more productive pace.

Distributed practice allows you to get rid of the metaphorical cobwebs,
and you accomplish more in the long run (and make fewer mistakes) and
feel more energetic and alert when you return to the task.

So the formula for successful and productive work is:

◆ **Don't keep on going hour after hour without interruption.**
◆ **Goof off a little every now and then and get rid of the lactic acid
and other fatigue products (chemicals) in your bloodstream.**
◆ **Work smarter — not harder or longer!**

❖   ❖   ❖

37. Inject Humor into Your Life

❖

*Nancy was telling her friend about an incident that happened several
years ago at a party. Nancy's husband got drunk and made a spectacle
of himself. "I was so embarrassed," she said, "and so angry that I was
practically ready to file for divorce. But then I saw the funny side of it.
This changed my anger into mirth and averted a needless confrontation."*

❖

Shared laughter forms an instant bond between people. Those who do not take life or themselves too seriously are much healthier and happier than those who do.

We aren't advocating a frivolous outlook, but people who are able to recognize the absurdities of everyday life and manage to chuckle about them are generally better able to handle and cope with stressful situations.

- **Attempt to take yourself lightly even when you are doing serious work.**
- **Try to laugh harder and more often. A genuine sense of humor enables one to keep out of mental ruts and can ward off boredom and even depression.**

What can be referred to as "mirthful laughter" is a psychic tonic. Biologists have hypothesized that laughter stimulates the production of catecholamines and endorphins in the brain, which affect hormone levels related to joy, and result in a higher pain tolerance threshold and a strengthened immune system.

Here are some ideas for lightening up.

- **Deliberately be on the lookout for more of the absurd, ludicrous and ridiculous events that go on all the time. See the funny side of them. Point them out to others. Keep a note of the funniest things you see or hear. This is sometimes called "Cosmic Humor."**
- **Even if something is not funny, try to laugh. You may be stuck in traffic, for example. Instead of scowling, try laughing. There is a theory that the shift in facial muscles may trigger some of the benefits of genuine laughter.**
- **Pay attention to whatever tickles your funny bone — cartoons, posters, letters, humorous stories, or jokes — and try to surround yourself with more of what amuses you.**

A word of caution. Avoid jokes based on ridicule. They are grounded more on hostility than humor and can inflict pain. And jokes based on cynicism are also not helpful and may in fact backfire. A play on words can be fantastic and really witty and amusing. Cultivate the capacity to appreciate life's absurdities.

❖   ❖   ❖

38. The Importance of Movement

❖

"I'm a natural born couch potato." Maurice said this with an air of resignation. Then he added, "I even remember finding every excuse in the book to avoid gym at school." Maurice needs to learn that strenuous exercise is not necessary for good health, but a brisk walk twenty or thirty minutes a few times a week would enhance his likelihood of wellness.

❖

The mind-body connection has been emphasized for many years and in various contexts. In short, what tones up the body also positively affects our mental, emotional, or psychological well-being.

Various experts have pointed out that many of us simply do not move our bodies enough. Something as simple as a five-minute walk before each meal can make an enormous difference. Activity increases your metabolic rate and burns calories which is all to the good.

- ◆ **You don't have to break a sweat in order to derive some benefit.**
- ◆ **Instead of taking the elevator, walk up a couple of flights of stairs.**
- ◆ **Stand up and move around while talking on the phone, reading letters, or thinking about a project.**
- ◆ **Suggest to friends that you go for a stroll.**

Opportunities abound for us to move our bodies. Put on a record and dance to it. Do some gardening. Deliberately park your car at the far end of a lot so that you have to walk some distance to shop. While waiting for your shower water to get warm or the bathtub to fill, do some push-ups or jumping jacks. If you enjoy jogging, or doing aerobic exercises, or if you can take twenty to forty minute brisk walks a few times a week, so much the better, but if not, even three to five minutes of movement or activity is better than none.

Research data show that even moderate physical activity such as walking elevates the metabolic rate and has many health benefits. The key is to think in terms of "activity minutes." What activity can I engage in rather than spend the time simply sitting around? Now we are certainly not recommending that you become obsessed about being active because rest and relaxation also have a definite place in a physical and mental health regimen. But if any of us errs, it will be on the side of too little movement and too much inactivity.

◆ **So turn off the TV, stand up, stretch, go out the door and move around a bit.**

There is no need to think of fitness in terms of dread and drudgery. Those who enjoy vigorous workouts will benefit from them, but if you hate working out, forget it. Simply inserting ongoing activity as we have described can be very beneficial.

❖ ❖ ❖

39. Taking Responsibility

❖

Delia played the "blame game." Whenever something was not to her satisfaction, she blamed someone else. She never asked herself if she had contributed anything to the situation. Even when clear-cut facts were brought to her attention, she refused to accept or admit any responsibility. Could this explain her failed marriage and general state of melancholy?

❖

It's amazing how many people deflect responsibility for their actions and choices and blame others or circumstances for their problems. While playing the "blame game" is common, too much deflection of responsibility is actually a self-defeating behavior pattern.

Those who insist on placing responsibility on factors beyond their control will tend to feel powerless and helpless. Only by accepting personal responsibility for our choices and actions can we enable ourselves to feel effective and more in control of our lives.

Taking responsibility doesn't mean that we have total control over our destinies. In reality we all are affected by events beyond our control such as our genetic endowments, and a host of random, environmental factors.

But within the vast currents of our lives and their surrounding circumstances, we can take hold of our personal rudders and steer our life course in specific directions. You must accept responsibility for your choices and behaviors.

Consider that blame and credit are opposite sides of the same entity. If we want to blame others for our misfortunes and problems, perhaps we should also give them credit for our successes and accomplishments. Likewise, liberty and responsibility are flip sides of the same concept; you can't have one without the other.

Dr. Victor Frankl, a renowned existential psychiatrist and concentration camp survivor, recently emphasized this point. Dr. Frankl commented on how odd it is that the United States of America boasts an impressive Statue of Liberty in New York harbor, yet no monument exalting responsibility exists to balance the privilege of liberty.

Just as Dr. Frankl believes that in San Francisco harbor a Statue of Responsibility should be erected to achieve this balance, so many of us need to accept our personal responsibility to balance the great liberty we all enjoy as citizens of this country.

◆ **Take responsibility for your actions and decisions and become the architect and engineer of your future.**

❖   ❖   ❖

40. *Don't Suppress Your Feelings*

❖

Natalie tended to bottle up her emotions. "I was taught to sit on my feelings," she explained. "In our family the girls were expected to smile sweetly and shut up." After a course of assertiveness training, Natalie started verbalizing her feelings. "It sure feels good to be a person rather than a doormat," she said.

❖

To continuously stifle feelings, to suppress all displays of anger or even irritation, to hide fears, or swallow annoyance is not healthy. Indeed, these suppressive tactics can result in dire consequences.

Of course, there are times when it is necessary or strongly advisable to suppress or hide true feelings. Only a fool would express his or her emotions at all times. The point is that

- when emotional inhibition is a habit, in time it becomes increasingly stressful to the individual, creating opportunities for health problems to develop.

The book *Emotion Inhibition and Health* edited by Drs. Harold Traue and James Pennebaker, addresses the age-old question: Does the inhibition of emotion have very negative effects on physical and mental health? Researchers in Austria, France, Germany, Ireland and the United States have shown that failing to express emotion can indeed trigger mental and physical problems, such as asthma (especially in children), headaches, psychosomatic complaints, and cardiovascular difficulties. So the question is: What's the best way of expressing feelings? If you are angry must you yell and scream and pound things? Emphatically not!

The best response is an assertive response, not an aggressive one. An assertive expression is simply saying things like: "That's annoys me! I hate it when you do that! I'm really scared of that! I feel very depressed right now!" Remember, don't deny your feelings and don't develop the habit of always hiding them from others. The bottom line is simple:

- **Don't suppress nor aggress, but do express your feelings.**

❖   ❖   ❖

BUILDING SUCCESSFUL RELATIONSHIPS

41. Keys to a Successful Marriage

❖

*Laura and Kyle went for marriage counseling. Laura was clearly upset.
"Kyle's on 'automatic NO!' " Then she almost sobbed: "Even if I ask
for a small favor it's 'No!' " Kyle retorted, "I don't think that's true,
but I'll tell you what is. Laura is forever finding fault with me and she
criticizes everything I do."*

❖

Unhappily married people, many on the verge of divorce, tend to make the same mistakes. They frequently express disapproval, are highly critical, blame, accuse, use threats, and are likely to say "No!" to each other a lot.

Such behaviors are killers of love and intimacy. When you are on the receiving end of criticism and blame from your spouse, the result is hurt and resentment. And when your partner refuses to grant reasonable requests, when he or she is on "automatic no," trouble is inevitable.

Most of the couples we see for marriage counseling make these errors. What is so remarkable is that they treat complete strangers politely, with tact, consideration and respect. Yet they dump on their loved ones. They incorrectly believe that home is the place to let your hair down, to be spontaneous and to drop any civility.

We are not advocating an inhibited, uptight marriage relationship. Openness and informality are two of the most important elements of a satisfying marriage. But keep in mind: Marital openness is not an invitation to attack each other with emotional napalm. Try instead to:

- ◆ **Express genuine caring, respect and consideration toward each other.**
- ◆ **Make deliberate efforts to please each other, and to avoid those things which displease each other.**

In our counseling sessions, we typically begin by asking each person "What kind, thoughtful and decent things have you done for your spouse this week?" Taking the other person too much for granted won't lead to conjugal bliss. A successful marriage requires some effort. But if the effort becomes hard labor, it probably signals basic incompatibility. *You have to work at marriage, but you shouldn't have to work too hard at it.*

And by the way, if you and your spouse are competitive with each other:

◆ **Remember that happy marriages are based on teamwork and cooperation, not on competition.**

Bottom line: If you want your marriage to succeed:

◆ **Avoid being critical.**
◆ **Try to say "yes" whenever possible.**

❖   ❖   ❖

42. How to Help a Troubled Relationship... or Make a Good One Better

❖

Like many busy professional couples, Jay and Georgia had drifted apart and almost lived in separate worlds. Nevertheless, they clearly cared for one another and needed to implement a direct and effective formula that would revive and nourish their marriage.

❖

As practicing psychologists we are often consulted by distressed couples or other people who are having various relationship difficulties.

Would you like to get your relationship back on track, or perhaps to keep life moving along more smoothly in a relatively trouble free relationship? In this segment, we're going to share with you four actions that you can take. While much of what we present here concerns marriages in particular, these same methods can be successfully applied to just about any intimate relationship.

Marital problems often stem from a decline of *friendship* within a marriage. Of course, there is an enormous variety of marital problems and any generalizations must be limited, but when partners lose their friendship, a downward spiral of marital unhappiness is almost certain to follow.

So, what can be done to nourish or revive the friendship in your marriage?

- *Compliment your partner* frequently. **Make a habit of saying something complimentary at least once a day.**
- *Express appreciation* **to your partner whenever he or she does something that pleases you.**
- **Make it a habit to** *do something thoughtful* **for your partner on a regular basis.**
- *Spend time together* **in mutually enjoyable activities.**

These kindnesses can be small but important things such as doing an extra chore around the house, or giving your partner an unexpected flower, or an inexpensive gift. After all, having a good time together is the very cornerstone of friendship ---- and happy marriages.

❖   ❖   ❖

43. Fight for a Successful Marriage

❖

Marilyn and Peter's problem was not that they tended to argue. They tore each other apart! Their arguments were vicious and extremely hurtful to both of them. Their painful, dirty fight tactics were destroying their marriage.

❖

Like Peter and Marilyn, you and your partner probably quarrel and have disagreements ---- that's human, after all. We hope, however, that your skirmishes don't result in open warfare! Keep in mind that the difference between happy and unhappy couples is not always *how much* they fight or *how often* they argue, but the *way they express anger and disagreement*. In fact, how you fight is one of the very best ways to diagnose the health of your marriage.

So, what can be done to safeguard your own marriage from the ravages of strife and friction? It's not a matter of avoiding arguments or conflicts ---- disagreements are inevitable. The key is to work at *resolving* them.

◆ **When you fight, avoid extremes of criticism, contempt, defensiveness, or withdrawal.**

◆ **Never fight by attacking your spouse — ask for a specific change in behavior.**

Extensive studies by Dr. John Gottman, a psychologist at the University of Washington in Seattle, have revealed some fascinating findings. Gottman has found what he calls "a magic ratio" between the amount of positivity and negativity in relationships. In good marriages the ratio is five to one. In other words, as long as a husband and wife express at least five positive feelings and actions for each negative message, the marriage is likely to be stable. (We strongly recommend Dr. Gottman's book, *Why Marriages Succeed or Fail.*)

Here's the bottom line:

◆ **If you want your marriage to be happy, show interest, be affectionate, show that you care, be appreciative, show your concern, be accepting... and fight constructively.**

❖　　❖　　❖

44. Can You Trust Her? That Depends...

❖

Gloria habitually made blanket statements about not being able to trust anyone. Her friend Karen never questioned anything or anybody. Guess which one frequently discovered someone had taken advantage of her?

❖

We frequently hear people say, "He can't be trusted," or "I don't trust her." What does that mean? Some people cannot be trusted with money. Others wouldn't steal a penny from you but wouldn't keep a secret. Someone else might be scrupulously honest with money and totally trustworthy in keeping confidences, but inclined to break promises or go back on his or her word.

Trust is, of course, a most important aspect of interpersonal relationships. The people we tend to gravitate to, those we select as friends and lovers are, we hope, fully trustworthy.

When one of our friends said, "I don't trust my husband," we assumed that she suspected him of having an affair and was deceiving her. However, it turned out that she meant that he would promise to fix things around the house and then make excuses. We are discussing a widespread tendency that creates enormous confusion and many misunderstandings.

◆ **Be specific unless you want to convey distorted impressions.**

Here's an example: You and Lucy are discussing the possibility of entering into a business arrangement with Harry. Lucy says, "I don't trust him." You wonder, and ask, "Why? What do you mean?" What exactly does she not trust about Harry? On the face of it, "I don't trust him" would seem to imply that the deal is off. But upon inquiry, let's say that Lucy is questioning whether Harry will invest his fair share of money into the venture. In this case, there's no need to scuttle the deal. What's needed is for Lucy to make her concern specific, and for Harry to agree in writing how much he is willing to invest.

This simple example shows the detours and vagueness that general statements can generate. We cannot say often enough: *please be specific*.

❖   ❖   ❖

45. How You Act Is More Important than Who You Are

*Myrna complained that her adult children treated her disrespectfully. When asked if she treated **them** with respect, however, she said: "I don't have to. I'm their mother."*

❖

Some people believe in unconditional love. No matter how obnoxiously they may act, they maintain that their closest relatives and true friends should continue to love them for "themselves." That's a mistaken notion.

Unconditional love is possible between parents and young children, but in most relationships:

- ◆ **Your conduct will determine who loves you, hates you, seeks you out, or avoids you.**
- ◆ **Take a hard, honest look at your actions and ask what you do for the important people in your life.**

Does your personality and your style make you lovable and ensure that your company is worth seeking?

- ◆ **Do you have a pleasant disposition?**

Are you easy to get along with? Are you helpful and obliging? Do you express affection? Do you show concern? Are you a good listener?

- ◆ **Or do you treat people badly?**

Are you petty, nasty, rude, impatient, or sullen? Are you generally critical? Do you often express disapproval? Do you often complain, make accusations, fly off the handle? Do you simply not pay attention to others? Even when you perform good deeds, do you do so reluctantly or unpleasantly? If you said "Yes" to any of these, don't be surprised if people distance themselves from you. Nobody can be sweet, warm, kind, loving, considerate, caring, and pleasant 100 percent of the time. The question to ask yourself is how often and under what circumstances you are selfish or uncaring. Remember, you reveal your love through your actions.

- ◆ **If you discover inconsistencies between who you are and how you act, you will need to change your actions. If you want to be treated nicely, you must act pleasantly towards others.**

❖   ❖   ❖

46. *Kindness Will Not Overcome Unkindness*

❖

Sally's husband was often abusive. One morning, over breakfast, Hank began yelling at her because she was on the phone instead of keeping him company. Later, after Hank went to work, Sally picked up his shirts from the laundry, ran some other errands for him, and decided to cook his favorite dish for dinner.

❖

Sally, alas, believed that if she could only create an ideal loving home atmosphere, her husband's abusiveness would stop. Unfortunately, she was in fact *rewarding* her husband's negative behavior. In response to his outbursts, Hank found his chores done for him and he was served his favorite dinner. Why would he change his treatment of his wife when she responds so positively?

The events that follow an action will weaken or strengthen the likelihood it will occur again. If Sally is nice to Hank when he treats her badly, she is teaching him to continue being abusive. By putting up with Hank's abusive behavior, Sally gives him the message that it's okay to treat her that way. If she showed him instead that she was willing to be especially kind and helpful *only when he was considerate and loving*, a positive pattern might be more likely to develop.

Tommy believed that kindness would overcome unkindness. He sent flowers to his wife whenever she flared up at him, hoping this gesture would put her in a good mood. Instead, it only encouraged her to flare up at him even more.

To encourage positive and discourage offensive behavior:

- **Do not reward behaviors in others that you wish to eliminate.**
- **Follow actor Alan Alda's advice: "Be fair with others, but then keep after them until they're fair with you."**
- **Learn to speak up.**
- **Do not reward unkind behavior from others.**
- **If someone treats you badly, say so — do not smile and pretend it's okay.**

❖   ❖   ❖

47. On Effective Parenting: Part 1

❖

*The Lintons really **tried** to be good parents. They seemed to think that if they provided adequate food, clothes and shelter, sent their children to church, taught them not to use foul language, and punished them when they stepped out of line, their parenting obligations would be satisfied.*

❖

Parenting is perhaps the toughest, most demanding, challenging and responsible job anyone can ever have. But there are no schools for it and no competency exams are required. It is strictly "learn by doing."

To practice in any profession where one provides services to the public, most states require a license or certification that can only be obtained by completing an appropriate amount of schooling and passing a competency test. Even marriage requires a license (unfortunately, however, a competency test is not a prerequisite!). Bringing another human being into the world requires nothing more than a pair of functional reproductive systems --- no training, no competency, no license!

Learning the crucial skills of parenting enables parents to be truly effective, increasing the chances that their children will be able to navigate the labyrinth of life successfully. One of the most valuable gifts you can give your children is a working compass (skills and facts) that can help them succeed in school and work, play and fun, love and intimacy.

Unfortunately, most schools do not include specific courses on how to acquire social skills, how to think rationally, how to control unwanted emotions, and how to be a truly effective parent. Parents must learn on their own how to resolve conflict, be assertive, and manage stress. And they need to discard the poor parenting techniques they may have learned from their own parents.

Of course all children are individuals and possess unique temperaments, needs and personalities, and there is no absolutely correct way to parent. Experts disagree on just what constitutes good parenting styles. However, in the next two segments we will discuss a few helpful hints and useful pointers that most experts do agree on.

❖ ❖ ❖

48. On Effective Parenting: Part 2

❖

Brenda came from a very permissive family, whereas her husband, Robert, grew up in a very strict household. They each had their own personal problems, but matters came to a head when they became parents. Their philosophies of child rearing were poles apart, and their kids were constantly caught in the crossfire.

❖

Children, of course, don't automatically know what's best for them, and parents must guide them in healthy and socially appropriate directions. The difficulty arises when parents pressure their kids to do what is really best for the parents, and not what is in the best interests of the children. There is a big difference between setting an 8 p.m. bedtime for a child who has a busy day the next day, and insisting on an early bedtime because the parents want to watch a television program.

Many parents see their children as extensions of themselves, and demand that their kids obey instructions without question. They don't recognize that children are free-thinking, autonomous individuals who can reason and act according to their own internal motivations. When parents are too demanding and overbearing, often the result is a child who is either rebellious and defiant, or one who is anxious and insecure.

♦ **Healthy ego development in a child requires that he or she have a voice in the family that is at least heard and acknowledged, if not necessarily agreed with.**

Overly permissive and indulgent parenting can result in equally unfortunate character development, including low frustration tolerance and feelings of excessive entitlement. As in most things, balance is the aim.

The key is to know when to be permissive and when to reign in the controls.

♦ **Imposing natural consequences for an action is permissiveness with a point.**

When Bobby refused to go to bed at 8:30, his father grounded him the next day. When Kenny insisted on staying up past his usual bed time, his father told him that no matter how tired he was the next day he would still have to mow the lawn after school. Grounding Bobby imposed an artificial consequence. It had nothing to do with bed time, and it probably injected an unhealthy dose of anger and resentment into their relationship.

But pointing out to Kenny that his choice to stay up late might result in his being too tired the next day to easily cope with his responsibilities allows the child to see a relationship between an action and the result, and better permits the child to learn from his mistakes.

❖   ❖   ❖

49. On Effective Parenting: Part 3

❖

Steve wanted to be a good father but he made a crucial mistake. He thought that if he insulted and verbally abused his children — telling them how stupid and inept they were — this would motivate them to prove him wrong, and they would get good grades and try to get ahead. Instead, he only succeeded in undermining their self-confidence.

❖

Being an effective parent is not easy. Parents "fly by the seat of their pants," and they often repeat the same mistakes with their own children that their parents made with them.

In fairness, it should be said that the tendency to blame parents for almost everything that goes wrong with their children is unfair and inaccurate. All of us inherit certain tendencies over which our parents have no control (they may give us our genes, but they can't change them — yet!). And the influence of peer groups can be more powerful than the benefits of even excellent parenting.

Nevertheless, good parents can make a difference by avoiding some of the main mistakes that uninformed parents tend to make. Less effective parents, for example, make their children feel guilty if they misbehave. In other families, a poor school report is made into a sin. A child who is made to feel morally wrong for some minor shortcoming may come to view herself as a bad person, and fail to develop an inner sense of self-acceptance: "You lazy bum, you'll never amount to anything! I told you to do the dishes before you went out to play!"

Poor parenting would have a little boy who runs into the street being chastised and called a "Bad boy!" A wise parent would issue a firm warning about the dangers of running into the street without attacking the child. It's more effective and less potentially harmful to make a clear distinction between what a child does and what he or she is.

- **Don't confuse inappropriate behavior with the basic identity of the child.**

Say, for example "*What you did* was naughty!" ⸺ not, "*You* are naughty!" There's a huge difference between calling a *child* stupid, selfish, or nasty, and telling him or her that a specific *action* was stupid, selfish or nasty.

Finally, consider this: If very minor infractions receive major penalties, what's left for parents to do if something really serious occurs?

- **Keep the punishment in line with the offense.**
- **Think long term: will my action help this child to grow up able to make healthy, independent judgements in his or her life?**

❖   ❖   ❖

50. On the Importance of Genuine Friendship

❖

Ted had become so involved with his work and family that he never made an effort to get together with his two best friends from high school and college days. He missed the closeness he had with them and felt a sense of loss in his life.

❖

"Friendship," goes an old saying, "is the best gift you can give yourself." Having one or two authentic friends adds a dimension to life that enhances emotional and spiritual well-being.

It seems to us that many people try to fill the need for friendship by having lots of *acquaintances*. But there are some important differences between being friendly with someone and having a genuine friend.

There's nothing wrong with having acquaintances, of course ⸺ people with whom you play tennis, go bowling, play cards, go out to eat, and so forth. But someone who says, "I have dozens of good friends," does not truly understand friendship! Real friendship is both a qualitative and a quantitative involvement. Our capacity for true intimacy is limited, so one cannot have a large number of *genuine* friends or there will not be enough emotional nourishment to sustain the relationships.

◆ **A certain amount of time must be invested into the relationship as well, since one key element of friendship is doing several mutually enjoyable things together.**

Friends have to be cultivated and friendship requires time and sincere effort. It also calls for risk-taking. You might want someone to be your friend, but he or she may not feel the same way about you.

◆ **Deep friendship is based on the development of love, and follows the rules of all intimate relationships.**

Women are often much better at fostering close friendships than men. Women share confidences and discuss their feelings — two necessary ingredients of friendship. Guys "hang out" with one another and tend to talk about things rather than emotions. Men are often inclined to try to have all their friendship needs met by their wives, often placing a burden on the marriage. Indeed, some people regard a good marriage as the ultimate friendship, and it may be, but we all need good, close, caring camaraderie aside from marriage.

◆ **The most fortunate people are those who are happy in a rewarding marriage or other committed relationship and, in addition, have one or two good friends.**

True friendship, like all intimate relationships, is based on similar values, sharing, caring, trust, respect, consideration, and balanced give and take without competing or "keeping score."

◆ **Anyone who can honestly say that he or she has two or three authentic friends is very wealthy in the emotional economy.**

Ralph Waldo Emerson offered this advice to those who would have genuine friends: "The only way to have a friend is to be one."

❖   ❖   ❖

COMMUNICATING EFFECTIVELY

51. Effective Communication

❖

"What's he look so fried for?" Burt wondered. "Jack said I could borrow his trailer. I would've gotten it back to him sooner, but I wanted to clean it up first. If he didn't want me to use it he should've said so!" Burt and Jack's communication breakdown could have been avoided if they'd used some straightforward communication skills: Jack's anger was actually due to a malfunctioning vacuum cleaner, and had nothing to do with Burt.

❖

Everyone communicates in one way or another, but very few people have mastered the skill of truly effective communication. Breakdowns in communication occur all too often and usually lead to a wide range of social problems, from hurt feelings and anger to divorce and even violence.

Communication is both an expressive, message-sending, and a receptive, message-receiving, process. Failure to communicate effectively can be due to a problem on either or both ends of the process.

Effective *expressive communication* can usually be achieved by sticking to a few important guidelines:

- ◆ **Make sure you have the attention of the person you wish to communicate with by establishing and maintaining eye contact.**
- ◆ **Try to send clear messages that are congruent in both verbal and nonverbal dimensions.**

To be congruent, make sure the tone and volume you use agrees with the content of the message you send: if you are pleased, look happy and sound happy; if you are angry, look annoyed and sound annoyed (but don't yell!).

- ◆ **Say what you mean and mean what you say. Be direct and honest; don't dance around the issue or play games.**

◆ Ask for feedback to ensure the message you sent was accurately received.

Effective *receptive communication* is based on good listening skills:

◆ Face the message sender and maintain eye contact.

◆ Nod, smile, or occasionally make affirmative vocalizations or other responses that tell the sender you're paying attention.

◆ Wait for the person to complete a thought without interrupting to express your own ideas.

◆ If you're not sure you understand the message, ask questions and seek clarification.

◆ Paraphrase what you heard so the sender can be sure you got the right idea.

By following these simple guidelines, you can improve your communication skills greatly, promote better understanding in your relationships, and enhance the quality of your life.

❖   ❖   ❖

52. Gender Differences in Communication: Fact or Fiction?

❖

"Men and women come from different planets and they will never learn how to communicate or speak the same language." Dina made this remark at a business luncheon. Her female colleagues agreed. Fred was less certain, but Jonathan said, "Even Freud never figured out what a woman wants."

❖

Recently a great deal of attention has been focused on how males and females differ in the way they use language. Books on the subject are being bought at an astonishing rate, and more and more people are beginning to believe that some unbridgeable communication chasm will forever hinder real understanding between men and women. The authors of these books maintain that gender differences in communication stem from biological, cultural, and social forces that have shaped the use of language into different forms for men and women. Some writers have gone so far as to suggest that the use of language is so dissimilar between the sexes that men and women may as well have come from totally different planets!

These authors assert that men use language as a tool for solving problems whereas women use language as a tool for increasing social intimacy. They maintain that men approach social and interpersonal relationships from the standpoint of hierarchy and dominance and tend to compete more than cooperate. Women are said to view relationships and social structure from the perspective of community and consensus and tend to cooperate instead of compete with one another. Thus, when a woman communicates a problem to a man, the typical male response is to try to solve it and he is likely to say, "This is what you can do about it." When a man expresses a problem to a woman, the typical female response is to try to empathize and she is likely to say, "How do you feel about it?" These basic differences are said to explain the majority of misunderstandings and communication breakdowns that plague many heterosexual relationships.

It is our view that while some of these assertions may be based on a thin layer of truth, like all generalizations and stereotypes, they crumble under the weight of individual differences. If a valid study of gender differences in communication has ever been conducted, we haven't seen it. Thus, there is no way to know how many men are basically non-competitive and nurturing and how many women are motivated by dominance and status. Indeed, those numbers are changing every day; the role women play in today's world and work force differs markedly from that which prevailed twenty years ago.

People are not slaves to their biology nor pawns on the elaborate chess board of society. Effective communication is a skill that can be mastered by men and women alike. When you come right down to it, we are all human beings and the psychological similarities between individual men and women far outweigh any real or imagined differences.

❖   ❖   ❖

53. Understanding the Elements of Communication

❖

"He never listens to me!" complained Alice. "Even when I'm trying to talk to him about something really important, like the kids, he just tunes me out." "I do want to talk about the kids," Tom replied. "It's just that she always waits until I'm doing something else, and then expects me to drop whatever I'm doing because she wants to talk."

❖

During waking moments, whenever we are in the company of other people, communication never stops. Everything we say or do transmits important information. For example, if Betty says to Tom, "I'm worried about Billy's poor grades on his report card," she is expressing a strong desire to discuss Billy's school performance. If Tom's response is to continue reading the newspaper, he is expressing an equally strong message that he is not willing to discuss the matter.

Many people run into problems with communication due to poor timing. "My wife usually wants to have a heart-to-heart discussion when I'm in the middle of watching TV." "The times my husband picks to talk to me are invariably when I'm on the phone with my business associates."

Communication is the process of exchanging information. It is the only means we have of understanding one another. In people who have no sensory or vocal limitations, oral or spoken communication is the most common way to express ourselves. Oral communication takes two forms: *verbal* ---- putting message content into words ---- and *nonverbal* ---- unspoken messages conveyed by actions (tone of voice, facial expression, gestures...). Messages can be positive or negative and can be conveyed through both verbal and nonverbal channels.

Another dimension of communication is the *context* in which it takes place ---- the circumstances in which the communication is occurring. For instance saying, "I'm going to take a walk," in the middle of an important conversation conveys a very different message than saying it when your partner is happily reading a book or watching TV.

Understanding these simple elements of communication and applying them intelligently can make an enormous difference to one's relationship.

❖   ❖   ❖

54. About Saying "No"

❖

When Roland asked to borrow Alvin's car because his auto was being serviced and he had an emergency, he was somewhat stunned when Alvin said "No." Roland mentioned that if Alvin ever needed to borrow his car, he'd gladly oblige. Alvin replied: "I made up my mind never to lend my car to anyone."

❖

Roland doesn't feel that he's just "anyone;" he thought he and Alvin were friends. Alvin may have legitimate reasons for not wanting Roland to take his car, but if he values his friendship with Roland, he needs to communicate clearly with him.

On a daily basis, many of the people who come to us for therapy reveal the negative consequences of arbitrarily saying "no."

Can you remember a time when you wanted something, made a reasonable request ---- asked a small favor, perhaps ---- and were told "no"? "No big deal," you say. Well, perhaps you can recall something that really *was* a big deal, something important to you that could easily have been granted but was withheld. Chances are that this denial left you unhappy, and not feeling very warm toward the person who denied the request.

Almost everyone has a negative reaction to arbitrary denials and refusals. When a reasonable and legitimate request is declined, when a simple favor is denied, most people feel hurt, angry, and disappointed. Depending on the importance of the event, some may become irate, outraged, or perhaps deeply depressed.

Both of us have seen people in our clinical practices who were "no-sayers," and whose lives were in turmoil as a result. When they realized that many of their relationship problems resulted from their negative styles, they saw the value of becoming more obliging and helpful, and their lives turned around.

Needless no-saying engenders a great deal of distress between partners, parents and children, employers and employees, teachers and students, friends, and so forth. So, when you are at the dishing out end of things, we urge you to

◆ **try to say "yes" unless there are valid reasons for doing otherwise.**

We're not saying that you should be a "yes person." There are legitimate times to refuse assertively to accede to another's demands. But if the other person is asking for something reasonable, and you value the relationship, try to say "yes." You may be surprised at how that enhances and strengthens the relationship.

By all means, say "no" when the time is right: if the request is unreasonable; if granting the request will cause harm to you or others; if granting the request will inconvenience you significantly. On the other hand, if granting a request or a favor is likely to be good for a relationship, will promote affection and goodwill, and won't hurt anybody, why not say "yes"?

❖   ❖   ❖

55. Letting Go of Grudges and Past Grievances

❖

Harold and Maude were in the office for their weekly marriage counseling session. Maude said, rather bitterly, "We were at a dinner party with my sister and brother-in-law and Harold made some outrageous remarks and really insulted them." Maude was visibly upset when recounting this event, and gave the impression that it was a fresh wound. Harold said: "What would you say if I told you this happened over eight years ago?"

❖

Maude was making a common but serious mistake, harping on a negative event from the past. It is never constructive to recite unpleasant things ---- however trivial or important ---- that your partner did to you in history. The past is dead and has value only in two ways: we can learn from past mistakes, and we can gain pleasure from recalling pleasant experiences from the past.

Rehashing unpleasant incidents or events creates distance and causes resentments, often leading to destructive arguments. If a deed was bad enough for you to end the relationship, so be it. But if you choose to stay together,

◆ **there's nothing to be gained for either of you by continuing to punish your partner for events in the past.**

If you want your partner to make up to you for the hurt, ask for what you want — firmly but pleasantly. To walk around feeling resentful will only eat away at you — and the relationship.

♦ **It's best to express it, resolve it, and drop it.**

Stop mentioning it. Neutralize your bad feelings. The first step is to downgrade the importance of the event.

Of course, you will want to consider what if any role *you* may have played in provoking an unpleasant incident. Ask yourself what you're accomplishing by harboring resentment. By hanging on to grudges and refusing to let them go, you only end up harming yourself and others.

It's worth noting that this discussion refers to grudges based on single isolated occurrences. *Patterns* are a very different matter.

♦ **If the issue concerns a repetitive and ongoing habit, active steps need to be taken.**

In cases of offensive or destructive patterns of behavior, you have every right to expect your partner to change this behavior. If not, you should seriously consider ending the partnership, particularly if any form of abuse is involved.

❖   ❖   ❖

56. The Dangers of Generalization

❖

When Eloise remarked that, "Mark is brilliant," she was referring to his clever strategies on the tennis court. Keith retorted: "Mark doesn't seem too smart to me." He was referring to the fact that Mark is not well-educated or intellectual. Both Eloise and Keith were generalizing.

❖

If Eloise had said that Mark is a brilliant tennis player, there would have been no reason for Keith to contradict her. Whenever you make a general statement about another person or about yourself, you are likely to be distorting the facts and conveying very little.

For instance, "You are selfish" or "You are wonderful," or "You are stupid," or "You are brilliant" is a vague generalization. "You are selfish," implies that the person always makes self-centered choices that disregard the needs and wishes of others.

Statements such as these tend to be made after specific events. For example, Gerald was annoyed that his wife revealed some personal information about his brother to several friends. "You're a blabbermouth!" he said. How much more effective it would have been for him to say, "I wish you wouldn't talk to your friends about my brother's problems."

Nobody is one way 100 percent of the time. If someone makes selfish choices 20 percent of the time, he or she is 80 percent *unselfish!* So it is best to be specific. "You acted selfishly at Sally's party when you refused to share that huge piece of cake with your friend Tommy." Similarly, instead of saying, "You're stupid," let him know what action is behind your criticism: "The comment you made to Ann about her mother seemed very silly to me."

◆ **Make your communications as specific as possible.**

Generalizations — "You're brilliant," "You're wonderful" — are usually false, and can cause embarrassment or even hurt. Someone can be wonderful with figures, brilliant with math but rather inept in other subjects. Thus, a statement such as "You have a wonderful vocabulary and a terrific way with words" conveys a lot more than "You are highly intelligent." And the same applies to general self-statements. "I'm foolish." "I never do anything right." "I am a genius."

◆ **Doing something selfish or stupid on occasion does not add up to being a selfish and stupid person.**

Conversely,

◆ **Doing something generous or brilliant on occasion does not add up to being a generous or brilliant person.**

And when you're on the receiving end,

◆ **ask others to be specific.**

If negative remarks are aimed at you, taking offense, or retaliating ("You are not so smart yourself!") is not nearly as effective as simply saying, "Can you please be more specific?" Most often, this leads the critic to rethink his or her position and state it in terms that are more constructive.

57. I-Statements

❖

"You never come home on time! You think that everything should run on your schedule, but the rest of the family can't always just wait around for you! Why can't you be more considerate?!" Sheila was sick and tired of nagging her fourteen-year-old son Ian about coming home late for dinner. But no matter how often she complained, he rarely was home on time, and usually they ended up arguing.

❖

How you say things matters as much as *what* you say. If you want to reduce needless tension and futile arguments, it will pay you to learn to use "I-statements" rather than "You-statements."

The difference between an I-statement and a You-statement is simple. Look at Sheila's tirade at her son: "You never... You think... Why can't you..." All You-statements. In contrast, I-statements go like this: "I get really upset when I've fixed a family dinner and you're not here on time."

Here's another typical example. A spouse says: "You're selfish and self-centered because you sit around expecting to be waited on and don't even help with the dishes." That's a You-message. Compare it to an I-message: "I would be very pleased if you helped me around the house, especially with the dishes."

Unless you are praising someone, You-statements are usually combative. Any complaint that starts with a *you* is often hostile. Even non-combative You-statements are very different from I-statements. Compare these messages. "You could call your mother more than once a month, you know" *vs.* "I think your mother would love to hear from you more often." Notice how the I-statement avoids any form of criticism. Which statement is more likely to gain someone's willing cooperation? Obviously the second, non-demanding one.

◆ **Use I-statements to express your wishes, and avoid critical You-statements.**

Here's another comparison: "Why don't you get off your butt and help me sort the laundry?" *vs.* "I'd love for you to give me a hand with the laundry." The basic formula is "I feel X when you do Y." "I feel all stuffed up and my eyes start burning when you smoke your pipe in the den." This is very different from, "How can you be so selfish? You know I hate it when you smoke your pipe in the den!"

Of course, even certain I-messages can be destructive. "I feel you are a moron!" is really a You-message disguised as an I-message. But the "I feel X when you do Y" formula merely let's someone into your feelings. For loving, pleasant, close and rewarding relationships, I-messages go a very long way. How often have you heard someone say: "If Johnny talked nicely to me I'd be more than willing to help him, but when he puts me down (by employing a *you*-message) I get totally turned off."

◆ **If you approach someone in a demanding, hostile, critical way, you are most likely to generate more heat than light — and gain very little cooperation.**

In clinical practice, we see the unfortunate consequences of combative communication styles on a daily basis.

◆ **People who routinely use I-statements tend to get along with others and are much happier.**

❖　　❖　　❖

58. On Empty Apologies

❖

If Greg felt wronged, he was perfectly satisfied if someone simply said "I'm sorry." These two words would get the offender off the hook. But he'd get really mad at anyone who refused to apologize. He seemed to think that the words "I'm sorry" had a magical quality to them. He couldn't understand why it seemed that so many people were taking advantage of him.

❖

Many people say: "You owe me an apology!" and become extremely upset when someone refuses to utter the two magic words — "I'm sorry." Frankly, it's hard to understand why so many people insist on hearing the words "I'm sorry." Many individuals find it simple to say "I'm sorry" over and over again without meaning it and without changing their actions.

If someone has hurt, upset, offended, inconvenienced, or otherwise acted badly,

◆ **it's best to make amends by *actions* as well as words.**

An apology is a good beginning, but the question to pose is, "What are you going to do about it now and in the future?" Too many people seem to believe that they can behave abominably as long as they're willing to apologize afterwards. They don't see the importance of refraining from repeating the same mistakes in the future.

Andrew, who had embezzled money from a friend, actually remarked, "Well, I *said* I was sorry!" Words are simply words: "I'm terribly sorry!" "Please forgive me!" Unscrupulous people can wring their hands in phony agony, express profound regret, and mean none of it.

In some cases, if a person is sincere, an apology may suffice. But instead of asking for an apology, a truly assertive person says "What can you do to be sure this will not happen again?"

That is crucial. It's easy to let someone say "I'm sorry!" but getting the offender to correct the misdeed is what's important.

◆ **Apologies have merit only if people also are willing to change their actions.**

Certainly, if you have acted in a way that someone found hurtful or offensive, it's a good idea (especially if you value the relationship) to apologize. Nevertheless, the bottom line is unchanged — apologies are words; and actions speak more loudly.

❖　　❖　　❖

59. Giving Criticism

❖

"I don't understand why she has to be so sensitive. I was simply trying to offer a little constructive criticism, but you'd think I just killed her cat or something." Mac's habit of criticizing others had just cost him another love relationship. Already once-divorced, he seemed to have trouble making friends, and his job was going nowhere.

❖

Most people are very sensitive and easily upset when it comes to receiving criticism. The process is a two-way street, shared equally between the person being criticized and the critic.

Even when criticism is constructively intended, the receiver may be overly sensitive and respond with feelings of anger, sadness, or guilt, especially when the criticism is delivered in a way that tends to arouse defensiveness such as sending it in the form of a You-message. (See Chapter 57 — "I-Statements.")

When people receive messages that start with You, such as "You didn't do this," "You never do that," "You always do the following," it is natural for them to feel attacked and take a defensive or even a retaliative position.

Fortunately, there are two excellent methods for giving constructive criticism that are unlikely to trigger bad feelings. The first is to

- **request a specific change in the future instead of pointing out something negative in the present.**

Instead of saying "You left the hall light on again," try saying, "In the future, please remember to turn off the hall light." Instead of, "I wish you'd stop wasting all of our money!" say, "In future, let's discuss our spending plans."

The second technique of constructive criticism is called the "sandwich method":

- **Sandwich the meat of a criticism between two positive comments.**

Instead of saying "You did a lousy job writing this report," using the sandwich method one could say "You did a great job on the introduction, but the middle section and conclusion seem a little weak. With a bit more work, I'm sure you can tighten it up into a really good report."

Giving criticism is a skill that, like all skills, can be mastered through learning and practice. It is often most helpful to request a specific change in the future instead of stressing something negative at present. "In the future, please remember to put your dishes in the dishwasher instead of stacking them in the sink." Requests go a much longer way toward achieving cooperation than snide remarks, put-downs and negative declarations.

It's also important to

- **decide if a criticism is really necessary *before* you offer it.**

Will the person being criticized really benefit from your comments? In Mac's case, he might be better off keeping his criticisms to himself. People are less likely to pay attention to criticism from someone who is a constant critic.

60. Receiving Criticism

❖

"It seems every time I turn around someone is complaining or griping at me," fumed Colin "My boss picks apart every report I turn in. My wife doesn't like the way I drive. The kids hate the food I cook." Colin's tendency to overreact to even minor criticisms caused him needless pain and suffering. A simple remark from his son David, "Dad, I don't like mustard on my hot dog," was met by a ten-minute tirade about "ungrateful kids."

❖

Who can go through life without being criticized? Nobody! Yet very few people know how to respond to criticism appropriately or how to deal with it effectively.

Basically, criticism can fall into three categories. It can be constructive, destructive, or irrelevant. Let's take a look at them.

Irrelevant criticism can best be ignored. Some individuals are so critical of everything and everyone that they will throw in critical comments that may have nothing to do with the situation at hand: "...and your sister has knobby knees." Irrelevant comments such as this are not worthy of a response, or of any emotional reaction on your part. In fact, ignoring them may encourage the criticizer to lighten up.

Destructive criticism usually comes in the form of an attack, a character assassination, a total put down. "You are a selfish pig!" "You are a disgusting person!" "You are stupid and incompetent!" If you are ever at the receiving end of such criticisms, try to realize that there is something wrong with the critic, with the person dishing out those remarks, not with you. A rational, sane, sensible person does not resort to extreme mud slinging. Whenever someone criticizes excessively, there is something psychologically wrong with him or her.

It is silly to take such criticisms to heart or to give them any credence. Rather, ask the critic to define his or her terms. "What is it exactly that makes you say I am stupid and incompetent?" The answer may sound something like this: "Well, you forgot to mail that important letter for me and you also made two errors when totaling the receipts for the day." An assertive person might respond that she or he had made some mistakes, but that does not make him or her a totally stupid and incompetent human being.

The positive note on this topic, *constructive criticism*, can be useful because it speaks to the issues. "I think you need to be more attentive. You omitted to mail that important letter and you made two errors when adding up the receipts." So if a criticism is constructive, learn from it. If it is destructive and you can do so without getting into deeper trouble, challenge the critic. If it is irrelevant, ignore it.

Many well-intentioned people, otherwise quite sensible and highly intelligent, have no idea how to give constructive criticism. They may also be unaware when being negative. Instead of recoiling with pain or taking offense, it may be useful to try to instruct such a person. Hal turns to Ron and says, "You are obviously a half-witted moron!" Ron inquires, "Hey Hal, do you know the difference between destructive and constructive criticism?" We do not expect Hal to roll over and say, "I apologize for insulting you. Please teach me how to change my style." It is sufficient to mention the difference between constructive and destructive alternatives. After delivering his rejoinder, Ron can walk away. If Hal is not half-witted, he'll get the message.

❖   ❖   ❖

61. Negative Emotional Language

❖

Alan and Claire had been dating steadily for several months before their first "real fight." They'd been to a party where Alan danced with Claire most of the time, but had also asked two other women to dance. "He was throwing himself at all the women! He wanted to dance with everyone but me," Claire exaggerated.

❖

There is a fundamental difference between descriptive language and emotional language. Emotional language tends to be very dramatic, strong, intense, and passionate. Descriptive language is rational, precise, and evident. It presents a simple, emotionally neutral statement about an event or a person. In descriptive language, George had danced with two other women. Period.

Using emotional language is fine when expressing positive feelings. "I love and adore you." "You are marvelous." But negative emotional language tends to damage relationships. "I hate the way you carved the turkey." "You said some awful things to my sister." It's best to be descriptive. "Next time I'd like it better if you'd try to carve the turkey thinner." "Let's try to get my sister to help out with chores; I don't think it helps to call her a spoiled brat."

We often encounter people who use negative emotional language and we try to show them how to change it into purely descriptive terms. Here's another example: John came home from work and found a note from his wife Rita, saying that she had gone to hear a lecture and was unable to make dinner. How did John describe it? He said, "She abandoned me; she just walked out and left me hanging." We replied: "You mean she went out one evening and expected you to make dinner for yourself."

Negative emotional language usually is accusatory and involves false inferences. There was no evidence, not a shred of proof, that George actually wanted to dance with "everyone but Claire." The more insecure a person is, the more likely he or she will use negative emotional language.

Obviously, when faced with patients who are insecure, considerable therapeutic work is necessary, but the first step is to encourage them to stop using negative emotional language. This aspect makes a big difference. If people remember to use descriptive language, they will have taken an enormous first step to overcoming needless insecurity and developing a better relationship.

❖   ❖   ❖

62. Assertion, Aggression and Passivity

❖

Artie's boss, Jonna, called him into her office to speak with him. "You've got to learn to control your temper." she advised. "I'm beginning to doubt whether I can trust you to act professionally around clients. It seems that you keep things bottled up until you can't hold it in anymore, and then you just explode."

❖

Many people think they are behaving assertively when they are really being aggressive or downright rude. And even though there are dozens of excellent books on "How To Be Assertive" and many people have attended assertiveness training seminars and groups, it's amazing how many still resort to the "bottle-up or blow-up" pattern of behavior.

Such people rarely respond to annoying matters as soon as they arise. Instead, they say nothing, stew on their feelings, add others to the list, and eventually, some minor event becomes the "last straw" and they let rip.

When you express annoyances as soon as they arise — keeping your life clear of resentments — your dealings with people are inevitably much better.

Many people erroneously think that minor events are not worth expressing. "Why make myself look so picky and over-sensitive?" they say. Others pride themselves on being "very private." They keep all their emotions locked up inside. This passivity is a serious psychological mistake. Such people are not only shut in, they are also shut out, because it's only by letting others into your feelings (positive and negative) that you can develop close and loving relationships.

◆ **If something significant is bugging you, get it off your chest.**
◆ **Be assertive about expressing positive emotions, too — love, appreciation, admiration, respect and gratitude.**
◆ **Become more of an emotional risk taker.**

Don't fail to express your feelings because of needless shame, embarrassment or fear. Let others into your feelings and see what a constructive difference it can make.

❖　❖　❖

63. On Being Extremely Private

❖

"Unlike many people I know, I've never gotten into trouble for shooting off my mouth," William boasted. "But now my girlfriend says she's tired of 'trying to pry information out of me.' I don't want to lose her, but can't she just get used to the fact that I'm a very private person?"

❖

What does "I'm a very private person" imply? Frequently, it means that the individual is closed in and has impenetrable walls around him or herself.

Most people grow upset when they feel someone has intruded or encroached on their personal domain. This reaction is quite normal and understandable. Part of democracy and freedom is the right to personal privacy. We want to be able to decide in whom we confide and what we entrust to them. Who would relish the idea of being spied on so that sensitive personal information becomes public knowledge?

Nevertheless, the desire for privacy can be taken too far. Some people always want to be seen in a good light. They go out of their way to hide shortcomings, covering their mistakes, and almost never saying what they really mean, because they want to be sure to please and impress others. Such people are apt to be tense, anxious, and suffer from poor self-acceptance.

It is truly amazing how far some people will go. They may literally be unwilling to answer a simple question such as "What did you eat for breakfast?" "What business is that of yours?" might be the retort. (That's one obvious or extreme example of a "very private person!")

◆ **In general, people who are not particularly secretive, who are open and willing to say what they mean and mean what they say, are psychologically healthier than their tight-lipped counterparts.**

But do not take as good role models those blabber-mouths who tell anyone and everyone their entire life history and instantly reveal their most personal feelings.

◆ **Try to be a little more open, to take the risk of letting others in.**

Open some gates and windows in your walls. You are entitled to privacy, but being too private can make you needlessly anxious and depressed. In addition, being too private is unlikely to invite close friendships and the give and take of love and sharing.

❖   ❖   ❖

64. The Virtues of Self-disclosure

❖

Penny had never told any of her new friends about the drug habit she had kicked over ten years ago. She was sure if they knew about it they would think less of her. But she felt like a phony and decided to risk opening up to them. "I can't believe it!" she beamed, "I thought it might really hurt my friendships, but instead it's made them better. Now they've told me more about themselves and we're much closer than before!"

❖

There are clear advantages to being more open and transparent. There can be no genuine love or close human interaction without shared intimacies and confidences. Life would be dull and colorless indeed without taking at least a few emotional risks.

Many have discovered that when they disclosed something personal, perhaps even shameful, others have said "I feel the same way," or "I did a similar thing." The resulting loss of isolation can be most heartening.

(Obviously, there are times when others are not entirely accepting. If censure rather than consolation follows a particular revelation, review and consider the discussion in Chapter 60, "Receiving Criticism.")

Too many people carry a guarded attitude into their friendships and other encounters, and they miss the joy that comes from sincere sharing. One of the best ways to acquire self-knowledge is to reveal yourself to trusted others and seek out their opinions.

We are not advising you to wear your heart on your sleeve, or to reveal your innermost thoughts and feelings to everyone. Some people are in fact potentially treacherous, and shouldn't be given the time of day, but it is usually not hard to determine who is trustworthy, who is for you and who might use information against you.

If you are accepted as people think you are, rather than as you really are, you will feel phony and insecure. It pays to build trust and intimacy by selectively expressing your genuine feelings.

Depriving yourself of the richness of intimate and loving relationships, by constantly hiding from others, leaves you feeling alienated from yourself.

♦ **To be loved for who and what you are (including your faults and limitations) instead of for some image you have created, is the path toward personal and interpersonal fulfillment.**

❖   ❖   ❖

HANDLING STRESS AND ANXIETY

65. Stress

❖

"Bryan, I'm not going to recommend any further testing at this point,"
Dr. Mullen stated. "Your physical symptoms seem to be occurring as a
result of stress. I am, however, going to recommend that you see a
therapist. You need to learn some stress management skills."

❖

Stress is a term that comes from physics and literally means pressure or strain that tends to distort a body. From a psychological standpoint, stress can be thought of as anything that challenges us to adjust or to cope.

Stress can come from our environments, from our bodies, or from our minds. Environmental stress might be caused by pollution, noise, or crowds. Bodily stress is caused by illnesses, injuries or straining the body in some way.

◆ **Most of our stress is caused by our negative thinking and faulty reasoning — creations of our own minds.**

While some stress can be good for us by helping to motivate action and solid performance, too much stress, over prolonged periods, can lead to physical and psychological problems. Many recent scientific studies have begun to uncover the wide variety of unhealthy effects that acute or chronic stress can have. There have been reports of people in Japan literally dying from overwork.

Problems ranging from high blood pressure, migraines, and stomach disorders to anxiety, depression, and panic, to name only a few, are often stress-related conditions. Some research even points to the possibility that certain disorders of the immune system are triggered by stress.

Since everyone is unique, there is no single best way to manage stress. Stress management programs must be tailored to individual needs, strengths, and limitations. Some people benefit from relaxation methods, some from exercise, while others do better with meditation and mental focusing techniques, or by learning how to identify and change stress-inducing thoughts and beliefs. But, many require a customized stress management package consisting of a variety of techniques. For you, the key point here is:

+ **Learn all you can about what causes stress in your life, and what works for you in dealing with it.**

We'll take a closer look at stress and what to do about it in the next few chapters.

❖ ❖ ❖

66. The Stages of Stress

❖

Rachel's friends agreed that she was strong-minded and successful. Unfortunately, her success was at the expense of her physical health because she did not pay attention to various signs that she was overtaxing herself.

❖

The first person to apply the term stress to physiological processes was the endocrinologist Dr. Hans Selye, who spent years studying the effects of stress on animals. Based on his work, Selye developed a three-stage model of stress called the "General Adaptation Syndrome" that is believed to describe the phases an organism goes through when faced with chronic or inescapable stress.

According to Selye, the first stage of the stress response is an "alarm reaction" that mobilizes the animal to take immediate and vigorous action to either escape from the stressor or do battle with it. This is commonly referred to as the "fight or flight" reaction and involves a very rapid and complex cascade of biochemical events that results in several stress hormones being pumped into the blood stream.

The next phase is called the "resistance stage." This occurs when the initial alarm reaction proves insufficient in dealing with the stress. During this stage, the body tries mightily to resist the onslaught of the stress by maintaining activity at a specific metabolic pathway that helps the organism cope by keeping the levels of certain circulating hormones high.

If the stress continues, the animal enters the final phase of the stress response, the "exhaustion stage." This occurs when the organism figuratively and somewhat literally runs out of gas. At this stage, it has depleted its physical, emotional, intellectual, and chemical reservoirs of energy and is just overwhelmed by the avalanche of unrelenting stress. During this exhaustion stage, the animal is most likely to suffer a variety of serious health consequences associated with chronic stress.

The upshot of this rather academic overview is simple:

♦ **Learn to manage stress before it damages your health and happiness.**

❖   ❖   ❖

67. The Pressures of Daily Living

❖

Ethan's job as a salesman was extremely demanding. "I'm going non-stop from the time I get there until I walk out that door. The crazy thing is, I feel like my home life is just as stressful. I don't know which is the 'frying pan' and which is the 'fire'!"

❖

Today, people are more than ever busy, pressured, constantly dealing with loose ends, knotted muscles, deadlines, nagging mistakes, fatigue, interrupted sleep, and financial headaches.

There once was a slower time when home was a haven, when people curled up with a good book, relaxed, unwound and derived the benefits of "home, sweet home." There was not much discussion of stress in those days.

Some people have more pressures and demands at home than at work — caring for children and coping with their busy schedules, errands, cleaning, yardwork, repairs, laundry, and worrying about making ends meet.

Others find it very difficult to leave work-related problems at the workplace. They are so immersed in their jobs that they experience great trouble letting go. Even when they do have a chance to relax at home, they are unable to do so. They cannot walk through the door, switch off their concerns about work and become a fully functioning parent or spouse. We advise our clients to avoid rushing home to listen to phone messages, jumping right into helping their kids with their homework, listening to their partners' gripes, or tending to domestic chores.

- **Most people need a "decompression period" when coming home after a day at work.**

To avoid the bends, you want your reentry into the home, after the day's compression at work, to be as gradual and easy as you can make it. Here are a few ideas for helpful and enjoyable relaxation inducers:

- **hop into a hot tub or take a warm relaxing bath or shower,**
- **lie down and have a short nap,**
- **listen to some of your favorite music.**

These simple measures can assist in leaving your worries behind.

If you buffer yourself against facing constant demands, you will replenish your energy and then be more able to attend to your chores. The time to talk about your hectic or frustrating day (or hear someone else's tale of woe) is after you've refreshed yourself like this:

- **sip a refreshing beverage,**
- **sit for a while on your balcony, deck, patio, den or other quiet space,**
- **take time for yourself,**
- **think about funny things that you have experienced,**
- **try to put a humorous or positive spin on the day,**
- **keep the tone positive by sharing the good news of the day first.**

❖ ❖ ❖

68. Avoiding Burnout

❖

"You've got to stop burning the candle at both ends!" Lorenzo's wife Sylvia warned. "The kids and I never see you, and the hours you're keeping are going to kill you!" Her prediction nearly came true: Lorenzo was forced to slow down when he landed in the hospital after collapsing at work.

❖

The term "burnout" is now part of our everyday language. It refers to those who overwork to such an extent that they become bored, exhausted, listless, unmotivated, depressed and even physically ill.

It doesn't take much for some people to feel burned out. We all react differently to stress, deadlines, pressures, demands, monotony and responsibility. What feels O.K. to one individual may be experienced by someone else as extremely irritating and disturbing. Nevertheless, there are specific tactics that everyone can follow to prevent burnout.

- Evaluate your goals and priorities. What do you really want to get out of life?
- Pursue other interests besides work.
- At work, try to do some things that have personal meaning.
- Become an active agent in making your life what you want it to be.
- Think of ways to bring variety into your work if at all possible.
- Attend to your health through adequate sleep, exercise, good nutrition and relaxation.
- *Never* jeopardize your health for any job.
- Learn specific methods to reduce stress on the job and at home.
- Learn to ask for what you want, but don't expect always to get it.
- If at all possible, delegate responsibility — don't take the entire load on your shoulders.
- Don't assume burdens that are actually the responsibility of others.
- Watch out for and get rid of any perfectionism in yourself.
- Learn your own limits and learn to set limits with others.
- If things are really tough, try to form a support group with colleagues to share feelings and to find a way of diminishing frustration.
- Learn to forgive yourself when you make a mistake or do not live up to your ideals.
- If necessary, consider seeking counseling for personal development or stress management.

❖ ❖ ❖

69. Panic Attacks

❖

"What's wrong with me?" Tillie wondered. She'd undergone a thorough checkup, but the doctor could find no medical reason for what was happening to her. "If nothing's wrong with me, then what in the world is causing these awful episodes? I can't breathe and it feels like my heart is going to burst through my chest!"

❖

You're feeling fine, minding your own business, when suddenly out of the blue you're gripped by an overwhelming sense of intense fear ---- you feel dizzy, your chest tightens, and you have trouble catching your breath. Your heart races, you shake, tingle, feel nauseous, and break into a cold sweat. Sounds like a heart attack, right?

Wrong! As surprising as it sounds, what has just been described is a *panic attack*. Panic attacks are often unpredictable, suddenly occurring, brief periods of intense fear associated with a variety of frightening physical symptoms. Many panic attack sufferers rush to the emergency room, convinced they have had a heart attack or a stroke.

Many people who have panic attacks cling to the false idea that they are really suffering from an undiagnosed (usually catastrophic) medical illness. The symptoms we described above (and many other negative sensations that accompany panic attacks) lead people to remain convinced that they are going crazy, or are about to drop dead. The first step is to persuade them that these terrifying thoughts are completely incorrect, and that their sensory discomforts are in keeping with the diagnosis of panic disorder.

As terrifying as it is, panic is actually a readily treatable condition that often responds to specific psychological therapy and only occasionally requires medicine. Indeed, numerous studies have shown that panic attacks can be rapidly and effectively treated by specific psychological methods.

If you have or someone you care about has panic attacks, don't suffer needlessly.

- ◆ **Seek help by contacting your family doctor or a qualified mental health professional.**
- ◆ **Learn corrective breathing and relaxation.**
- ◆ **Learn to re-label the physical sensations of the panic as manageable and nonthreatening instead of catastrophic.**

♦ **Learn to reduce panic symptoms by intentionally triggering them in controlled situations.**

If untreated, panic attacks often get worse and can lead to a condition known as "agoraphobia" (literally "fear of the marketplace"), an emotionally crippling anxiety that results in ever-increasing patterns of avoidance and confinement.

❖   ❖   ❖

70. *Obsessive-Compulsive Disorder*

❖

Louis set the alarm clock each weekday for 5 a.m. although he did not have to be at work before 8:30, and only lived a few blocks away. He was plagued by various rituals that took hours to perform each morning. He felt compelled to start with elaborate cleansing activities followed by checking, arranging and rearranging scores of household items.

❖

It's perfectly normal to check things once or twice, to see that the doors are locked, the stove has been turned off, the alarm clock has been set, and to occasionally worry about whether or not various tasks have been adequately or safely completed.

Some people, however, spend so much time repeatedly checking and re-checking things, and experience such intense worry and anxiety if they don't, that their compulsions seriously interfere with their lives and emotional well-being. These folks may be suffering from a condition known as Obsessive-Compulsive Disorder ---- OCD.

Obsessions are intrusive, recurrent and persistent ideas, thoughts, impulses or images that often seem frightening and senseless and tend to create high levels of anxiety.

Compulsions are repetitive and intentional behaviors that are performed in response to an obsession, or according to certain rules, or in a ritualistic fashion. The purpose of the compulsion is to neutralize or prevent anxiety or some dreaded event or situation.

Most of the time OCD sufferers recognize that their compulsions are irrational or excessive, but, nevertheless, feel powerless to resist or stop them.

OCD takes many forms. In addition to obsessing about safety or responsibility, and thus checking things compulsively, some people obsess about dirt, germs, contamination, or disease and consequently wash or clean compulsively. Others obsess about having blasphemous or undesirable thoughts. Often people perform rituals involving counting, arranging, or touching things according to specific rules.

OCD used to be considered a rare and bizarre condition. It is now known that it's tragically common, affecting millions of people. Fortunately, recent advances in the medical and psychological understanding of OCD have led to very successful treatments for it, usually a two-prong approach involving specific medications and highly specialized behavior therapy.

Like clinical depression,

◆ **OCD is best thought of as a treatable illness, a metabolic disorder of brain chemistry, not as a weakness or a personality defect.**

◆ **You are urged to seek professional help if this condition is disrupting your life.**

❖   ❖   ❖

71. *Generalized Anxiety Disorder*

❖

"I'm very good at worrying." Greta said, "If they gave a prize for being the biggest worrier, I'd win for sure." Her family used to tease her about being a "worrywart," but lately her anxiety was getting out of control: she couldn't sleep, her heart raced, her stomach was often upset, and yesterday she'd nearly passed out from dizziness.

❖

Everyone experiences anxiety from time to time. It's perfectly normal to worry about things on occasion and to even feel physical reactions in connection with the worry. Some people, however, worry so much and experience such intense physical symptoms associated with their worry that it becomes a real emotional handicap that prevents them from leading happy and healthy lives. These "worrywarts" may be suffering from a condition known as Generalized Anxiety Disorder ---- GAD.

GAD is characterized by two major components. First is *unrealistic or excessive worry or anxiety* about a number of events or activities, such as possible misfortune to a loved one who is in no danger, or worrying about finances or job security for no good reason. In the case of children and adolescents, this disorder may take the form of anxiety and worry about academic, athletic, or social performance.

The second major component of GAD is a variety of mostly *physical symptoms* that are often present during periods of anxiety. These include feeling shaky; experiencing muscle discomfort; restlessness; and tiring easily. Other GAD symptoms involve difficulty breathing; rapid heart rate or palpitations; sweating or cold, clammy hands; dry mouth; dizziness or lightheadedness; gastrointestinal disturbances; hot flashes or chills; or frequent urination. The last group of GAD symptoms include feeling keyed up or on edge; excessive jumpiness; concentration or memory difficulties; trouble sleeping; and irritability.

To qualify for a diagnosis of GAD, at least three of these symptoms must appear during periods of worry and the person must have been bothered by them more days than not for a period of at least six months.

Fortunately, most GAD sufferers can be helped by specific cognitive behavioral therapy methods. In some cases medication may also be helpful. Once again, our advice for dealing with this debilitating condition is simple:

◆ **If the symptoms of GAD describe you, get professional help.**

❖ ❖ ❖

72. Conquering Anxiety

❖

Carlos tended to dwell on all the things that could possibly go wrong. His wife commented that Carlos would spot danger where none existed, and had taken to calling him, "Don Quixote." His imagination would often conjure up perils that most people would never even begin to consider. Carlos said of himself, "I think I must be crazy."

❖

Carlos suffered from a treatable anxiety disorder. There is a lot of diversity among anxiety disorders, but most appear to be rooted in a common soil of unrealistic or excessive worry about various events, situations, or circumstances.

Most anxiety-producing concerns involve a particular style of thinking that usually starts with "what if..." thoughts that trigger or increase anxiety, especially when the imagined concern — the "what if..." — involves a significant threat, misfortune, or catastrophe.

Related to these "what ifs" are often equally catastrophic mental pictures or images. Since the mind and the body are different sides of the same coin, thinking calamitous "what ifs," while simultaneously visualizing similar misfortunes, is one sure-fire way to rev up the emotional machinery of high anxiety.

Indeed, most people can induce anxiety by thinking of and picturing threatening, unfortunate, or catastrophic events. But, that also means we have the power to reduce or even prevent excessive anxiety by turning around our thoughts and mental pictures.

- **One of the best ways to turn the tables on anxiety-creating "what ifs" is to either add the word "so" to the beginning of the thought or to counter the "what if" idea with a calming "well then" response.**

Thus, *"What if* X,Y, or Z happens"* becomes *"So what if* X, Y, or Z happens."* Or, *"What if* A, B, or C happens"* is immediately followed by *"Well then, 1, 2, or 3."*

For example, *"what if* I fail the test"* becomes *"so what if* I fail the test,"* or *"well then,* I'll study harder next time."* And *"what if* I say something foolish"* becomes *"so what if* I say something foolish"* or *"well then,* I'll feel a moment of embarrassment,"* and so on.

- **By thinking calming thoughts and visualizing positive events, you can rapidly ratchet down the intensity of just about any anxiety reaction.**

But keep in mind that anxiety management skills, like all skills, take learning and practice to master.

❖   ❖   ❖

73. Putting Anxiety in Its Place: Risks vs. Resources

❖

Franklin was a good accountant and had a well-paying job, but when he calculated various emotional risks, his figures were all wrong. "There's no way I could ever ask Denise out," he thought to himself. "I'd probably stumble all over my words, and she'd think I'm a jerk. I could never show my face around her again."

❖

The uneasy feelings of anxiety are usually due to some misfortune or dreaded event that people expect or anticipate — a sense of threat or of being at *risk* for suffering some loss or injury.

The amount of *resources* that people feel they have for coping with the risk also figures into anxiety experiences. Usually, when people feel extremely anxious, they tend to overestimate the risks and underestimate their ability to deal with them.

Here's an example that helps to illustrate this point: Imagine you're camping in the deep woods, sitting by a fire, when suddenly, out of the trees a large, ferocious and very hungry bear appears. On a scale of one to ten how scared will you feel? Probably a *ten*, right? O.K., let's assume you have a strong, long and sharp stick to fend the bear off with, now how anxious will you feel? Maybe a *nine*? What if you were with a large group of people, all with sharp sticks? What is the fear now? Or, let's say instead of sharp sticks, the group was armed with burning torches? What's the level of fear now? Perhaps a *six*? Let's go a step further and assume the group had rifles and shotguns. How frightened would you feel then? Probably much less than a ten, a nine, or a six, right? Sure, because in this last scenario you perceive yourself as having powerful resources (guns) for coping with the risk (a bear).

Of course, on our imaginary camping trip, we would merely fire a few blanks into the air and the bear would run off unharmed. (Never fire live ammunition into the air — it will come down somewhere!)

The point here is to underscore the relationship between our appraisals of risk and our estimates of coping resources and how this relationship influences anxiety experiences. Remember, most anxious people overestimate the risk or threat and underestimate their coping resources. Franklin probably would not make a jerk of himself in asking Denise out, even if she turned him down. What's more, he very likely has the personal strength to recover with only a few "scars" if she did say "no."

The next time you start to feel anxious,

♦ **ask yourself if you are accurately gauging the extent of the risk you're facing and then try to consider all the resources you have at your disposal for coping with it.**

We believe this simple exercise will be very helpful in keeping a balanced perspective and can assist you to reduce unnecessary anxiety.

❖　❖　❖

74. Hyperventilation

❖

"Jeez, Maddie, you're panting like a dog! What's wrong with you, anyway?" Maddie's brother David wasn't the first to notice her strange breathing patterns. The odd thing was, Maddie never noticed that she was doing it until someone else brought it to her attention. "Maybe that's what is causing those dizzy spells I've been having," she reasoned.

❖

Improper breathing can leave you breathless! Don't hold your breath. Read on to understand the impact of hyperventilation.

Breathing is one of those functions we simply take for granted. After all, breathing is a natural reflex that seemingly takes care of itself without conscious thought. Nevertheless, many people breathe improperly and may therefore be prone to the hyperventilation syndrome.

Every time we exhale, we expel carbon dioxide (CO_2) from our lungs. This is good because if too much CO_2 builds up in our bodies it can be unhealthy and result in unpleasant symptoms. But expelling too much CO_2 can also produce a wide range of scary sensations and symptoms such as dizziness, shortness of breath, heart palpitations, tingling, numbness and excessive sweating.

Some authorities maintain that the hyperventilation syndrome (HVS) happens because CO_2 is dissolved in our blood in the form of carbonic acid. When too much CO_2 is released from our bodies, the concentration of carbonic acid in our blood drops and the body furiously struggles to compensate, thus causing the symptoms of hyperventilation.

◆ If you often experience unpleasant dizzy spells, shortness of breath, heart palpitations, tingling, and the other symptoms referred to above, you may be suffering from HVS.

The first thing to do is

◆ see your family doctor to rule out any obvious medical conditions.

If symptoms continue, try the "paper bag" method. Here's what to do at the next episode:

◆ Try taking five to ten breaths into a lunch-sized paper bag (always use a paper bag — never a plastic bag) recycling the same air over and over.

This should increase the CO_2 levels and restore the carbonic acid balance in the blood, thereby reducing symptoms. Other methods, all simple but effective, are slow abdominal breathing and the technique of running in place.

◆ If symptoms persist, consult your family doctor again, or see a health or mental health professional who specializes in therapeutic breathing techniques.

❖   ❖   ❖

75. Multiple Personality Disorder

❖

"What a beautiful necklace, Julie!" Ida exclaimed. "Wherever did you get it?" Embarrassed, Julie told her Aunt Ida that she had no idea where the necklace had come from. In fact, for the past few months, there had been instances where she could not account for periods of time. Ida, knowing of her niece's traumatic childhood, immediately suggested that Julie see a therapist.

❖

Perhaps one of the most controversial and potentially dangerous psychological diagnoses is the so-called "Multiple Personality Disorder" (MPD), which was recently reclassified as "Dissociative Identity Disorder" (DID). Briefly, MPD or DID involves several features, chief of which is the presence of two or more distinct identities or personality states, each with its own enduring pattern of thinking, perceiving and relating.

In suspected cases of MPD or DID, at least two of these identities or personality states recurrently take control of the person's behavior and the individual is unable to recall important personal information that is too extensive to be explained by ordinary forgetfulness. In the vast majority of these cases, there is a reported history of extreme anxiety, usually stemming from traumatic abuse or neglect.

The fact that the mental health establishment reclassified MPD as DID indicates that the very concept of the disorder is unstable, open to debate, and hard to pin down. Unfortunately, there are some mental health practitioners who seem almost married to the diagnosis and claim that dozens of their clients are suffering from the condition. In truth, if MPD or DID even exists, it is amazingly rare.

The danger for the consumer is that if a therapist unquestioningly buys into the label, the therapist will be likely to find, or worse yet, manufacture, evidence that supports the diagnosis. Even more alarming is that some clinicians actually encourage behaviors that seem consistent with the label, which increases the likelihood that the client will act more like the label and begin to "fit" into this diagnostic category.

We are not denying that people can have strange, disconnected, amnesic and fragmented experiences, nor are we totally decrying the diagnosis of MPD or DID. It is possible that some unfortunate people who suffered through horrendous abuse, neglect, or trauma may indeed suffer from this condition.

Nevertheless, before placing the label MPD or DID on someone, other more rational explanations for the behavior must be ruled out, such as medical conditions, drug intoxication, or perhaps more credible psychological disturbances such as Post-traumatic Stress Disorder. The bottom line:

   ◆ **MPD or DID is not a widespread or common disorder despite the insistence of some practitioners.**

❖   ❖   ❖

DEALING WITH DEPRESSION, ANGER AND MOODS

76. Depression

❖

Dawn had been feeling extremely depressed for months. But, because she felt that she had no reason to be depressed, she was embarrassed to tell anyone how she was feeling. She put on a happy face in front of her friends and family, and continued to suffer alone.

❖

Almost everyone gets the blues from time to time —— that feeling of sadness or grief that usually results from unpleasant life experiences. While many people refer to the blues as depression, however, true clinical depression is as different from the blues as pneumonia is from a case of the sniffles!

The blues is a temporary and usually normal reaction to stressful life situations. Most cases don't involve physical symptoms, loss of self-esteem, or suicidal thoughts, and the negative state usually passes within a few hours or days.

Depression on the other hand, is an intense, pervasive and long-lasting disorder of mood that attacks the body as well as the mind, often resulting in serious problems in work, social, and physical functioning.

Symptoms of depression often include disturbances with sleep, appetite and body weight, energy, concentration, and sexual functioning. There is frequently excessive guilt, feelings of worthlessness, loss of interest or pleasure in activities, and, in severe cases, thoughts of —— or attempts at —— suicide.

Unfortunately, some people don't recognize depression for the serious illness it is. They think of it as a personality flaw, a sign of weakness, a character defect, or, perhaps, a temporary blue mood.

The fact is, clinical depression is an illness, not a weakness or a passing blue mood. Depressed people cannot simply "snap out of it" or just "pull themselves together," any more than a diabetic can merely snap out of a blood sugar imbalance. And, without appropriate treatment, symptoms can last for months or even years.

Some depressions are the result of a chemical imbalance and may only be treated by anti-depressant medication. Some require psychotherapy, and still others a combination of methods.

The good news is that

◆ **more than eighty percent of depression sufferers can be treated successfully.**

If you, or someone you care about is depressed,

◆ **seek help now by contacting your family doctor or a qualified mental health specialist.**

❖   ❖   ❖

77. Anger

❖

"You're lucky that kid only flipped you off, Wally!" his wife screamed as the other car sped away. "He could have pulled a gun out instead!" Wally knew Sandra was right. His inability to control his anger was destroying his life: no one in his family would speak to him except his mother, and he'd recently been fired from his third job in six months. What Wally didn't realize was that his anger was actually affecting his physical health.

❖

Anger is the most destructive emotion ---- more damaging than depression, anxiety, or guilt feelings.

You may have heard the theory that people who display so-called "Type A" behavior ---- often rushing, impatient, hard-driven, and over-ambitious ---- are at greater risk for heart disease than people with "Type B" characteristics ---- those who are more laid-back, easygoing and unhurried.

Well, further studies showed that the problem or the killer was not due to the pace, the pressure, or the hard-driving qualities of Type A behavior, but that these personalities were usually very *hostile*, and that anger was at the root of it.

The destructive impact of anger on a person's physical and mental health has now been well documented. But where does anger come from? How is it generated? The simplest answer is that we create anger by placing demands on ourselves and others.

It's the theme that crops up time and again — the impact of shoulds, oughts and musts. Anger always entails a should. "You *should* have known better!" "You *shouldn't* have been sassy to your Uncle Charlie!"

- ◆ **Shoulds and should nots — the more you have, the angrier you will be.**

Unless you are Jehovah and run the universe, you really don't know what "should" and "should not" occur. You know what *you* would prefer, what *you* desire and wish for, and what *you* think is right and wrong, good and bad.

To say: "I think it would be nice if you did more work around the house" is very different from "You should do more work around the house." Why *should* anybody do anything? The point is that *you would appreciate it* if certain things were done, or perhaps done differently.

But that doesn't mean that anyone should obey your wishes and that it makes sense to get really mad at them if they don't.

- ◆ **Give up your shoulds, stop laying them on others, and see what happens to your emotions.**

You will definitely experience less anger, and you may live a longer, healthier and happier life.

❖   ❖   ❖

78. More Facts about Anger

❖

Karl commented that the things a person gets angry about can tell you more about him or her than anything else. "I once dated a woman," he said, "who got really angry when I sent her roses." It turns out she did not like roses and felt that Karl should have checked with her first. "She was so mean and petty about it, and she completely missed my good intentions. I knew that this meant big trouble, so I ended the relationship." Karl added knowingly, "I heard she just got divorced for the fourth time."

❖

Anger is a very common experience and emotion. For some, hardly a single day goes by without experiencing anger. It can be expressed outwardly, or it can be held in. It can be controlled or uncontrolled. It can persist or it can be resolved.

Often, expressed anger leads to alienation from others. People who fly off the handle also often suffer from a negative self-concept and poor self-acceptance.

Anger is behind a good deal of interpersonal conflict, occupational failure, domestic and family strife. It can escalate into hostility, fury, rage and even result in murder. Anger that is held in or suppressed may be related to medical conditions, such as high blood pressure and coronary artery disease.

But *how* you express anger is important. People express their feelings of anger differently. Some sulk, others yell, or glare, or make snide remarks, or withdraw. In the 1970s, it was fashionable for therapists to tell their angry clients to "let out" their anger by beating a pillow and screaming, or to hit someone or something with a soft foam bat, but these actions only resulted in even greater levels of anger, and are not recommended by knowledgeable professionals today.

It's also important to note that

◆ **anger is not synonymous with aggression; anger is an emotional state, aggression is a behavior.**

Aggression includes a deliberate intent to harm, hurt, or injure another person, or do damage to an object.

Is there such a thing as "verbal aggression"? Many authorities say that aggression is best defined as physical behavior with the goal of contact ---- shoving, hitting, punching, etc. Nevertheless, in many unstable persons, even a verbal remark such as "You're a jerk!" may be considered aggressive, and can result in an aggressive response.

It has been shown that making an angry face will actually induce a person to feel angry, whereas putting on a "happy face," smiling and acting happy, has the opposite effect.

Today, effective anger-reduction programs include exercises that work toward these goals:

- ◆ **increase your overall level of happiness,**
- ◆ **learn to relax fully,**
- ◆ **learn to "let go" of unimportant anger triggers,**
- ◆ **learn to express justified anger in assertive — not aggressive — ways.**

Finally, as we have said on many occasions, behind all anger lies a *should, ought,* or *must.* We cannot say this often enough.

- ◆ **The fewer should, oughts or musts you have the happier you and all those who associate with you will be.**

❖   ❖   ❖

79. Is It Healthy to Blow Off Steam?

"So how's your love life?" Samuel's sister, Trisha, asked. Samuel blew a gasket. Red in the face and shaking all over, he slammed his fist on the table and yelled, "Get out of my face!" This was typical behavior for Samuel. He would usually apologize later, saying that, "If I held it in, I'd just end up having a heart attack."

❖

Let's get to the bottom line immediately.

- ◆ **Flying off the handle or blowing off steam when angry is not healthy.**

When someone loses his or her temper and lets it rip, everybody loses. But to deny or suppress angry feelings is also inadvisable.

♦ **Doing little more than smiling sweetly when you are angry is also unhealthy.**

You need to express your anger, but there are healthy and unhealthy ways of doing so. If you suppress your anger, if you displace it, deflect it, deny it, ignore it, disown it, or project it, trouble is likely to result. The basic rule is to:

♦ **Express your anger, but do so appropriately with direct statements, rather than angry tirades.**

"I'm angry that you insulted my brother in public." That's a simple and direct assertive statement. That's what we mean by the appropriate expression of anger. "Oh come on!" you may be saying. "That's so weak, so wimpy, so mealy-mouthed." To get the anger out, some people believe that it is necessary to raise your voice, stomp your feet, holler, scream and really tell someone off.

In truth, when people vent their anger, when they explode, they cause damage — often to their own health, and they also tend to lose the recipient's respect.

A widespread myth leads many people to assume that forces and pressures build up in the nervous system, and unless they are fully discharged, blood vessels can literally break. In fact, the opposite is true. If you blast off like a rocket or bellow like a mad bull, you put quite a strain on your cardiovascular system.

Parting thoughts about anger:

♦ **Losing your cool puts you at a disadvantage. If you get enraged it only shows how much power other people have over you.**

♦ **When you are angry, it pays to express yourself assertively and not aggressively.**

❖ ❖ ❖

80. *Don't Upset Yourself about Upsetting Yourself*

❖

"I'm such an idiot!" Linda said through gritted teeth. "Why do I always let my mother get me so irritated? You'd think I'd be used to her sniping by now." "Oh come on!" her friend Sherry replied. "What are you supposed to be, a saint? That woman would get on anyone's nerves!"

❖

Many people realize that they are being needlessly anxious, or angry, or otherwise upset over certain events. They ask: "Why do I let these stupid little things bother me so much?" and then they criticize themselves for being so "weak" or so "stupid" as to bring it on.

As a result of this self-criticism, they suffer not only from the original anxiety, or depression, or anger, or guilt but, on top of it, they also suffer *because they are suffering.*

So they make themselves depressed about their depression, anxious about their anxiety, angry about their anger, guilty about their guilt, and generally lapse into self-pity.

Peter has a very demanding boss who constantly berates him unfairly and he hates himself intensely for being angry at his boss.

Sally is unassertive with her friend Carol, and is angry at herself for letting Carol get away with too many put-downs.

Are disturbances about disturbances important? Indeed they are.

If Peter wastes time and energy about being angry with his boss, he will tend to be so absorbed in his self-denigration that he will devote less time to what he needs to accomplish — how best to deal with his boss. If Sally remains angry at herself for being unassertive, her own anger will diminish her chances of developing the social and other interpersonal skills she needs to acquire.

- ◆ **The first step in correcting this is to take a careful inventory of yourself.**

If you feel depressed, or anxious, or otherwise upset, ask yourself if you are also depressed about your depression, or anxious about your anxiety. If the answer is "yes,"

- ◆ **accept the fact that, as a human being, you have the right to feel the way you do without making yourself guilty on top of it.**

Say to yourself: "I certainly would like *not* to be anxious or depressed, so instead of dumping on myself and giving myself a hard time, I'll try to remedy the real situation."

You need to realize that

- **being anxious when there is no real danger is futile and unwise, but that does *not* mean that *you* are a foolish person.**
- **Don't allow yourself to believe that it's okay to treat yourself poorly as long as you are kind and forgiving to others.**

Remind yourself:

- **You're a person and you deserve kindness, even from yourself.**

❖   ❖   ❖

81. Mood and Variations: Opus 81

❖

Eliot looked troubled. "I think I'm a manic depressive," he declared. "Why do you think that?" Eileen asked, "You know that everyone has ups and downs." "Yeah," Eliot continued, "but it doesn't make any sense... some days I feel happy and glad to be alive, and on others I feel really down in the dumps."

❖

Everyone is moody from time to time. It's psychologically impossible ―― and even undesirable ―― to be constantly on an even keel. A head of cabbage experiences no fluctuations in mood, but human beings are subject to many nuances in their feelings and emotions.

During the course of a single day, you might experience many moods, both positive and negative. You may feel sad, insecure, nervous, annoyed, disgusted, frustrated, irritated, and disappointed, as well as proud, excited, happy, cheerful, and loving.

That's a list of normal, everyday mood variations. But suppose that instead of experiencing some annoyance you became enraged, and in place of some slight nervousness you felt panicky ―― then you would have entered a potentially abnormal area. The *intensity* of the reaction is an important aspect of mood.

There is a large difference between normal sadness and abnormal depression, between happiness and pleasure and undue elation and extreme euphoria. People who have been successfully treated for depression often grow concerned when they feel blue or down in the dumps until they learn to distinguish between depression and normal melancholy.

Thus, while ups and downs in moods are normal and to be expected,

+ **watch out for moods that are unduly intense and prolonged.**

Generally, moods can be tied to circumstances or situations. "I'm disappointed and in a bad mood because my date didn't show up and I was looking forward to a pleasant evening." But the person who says "I'm crushed, humiliated, ashamed and deeply hurt because my date didn't show up" is expressing abnormal reactions.

Apart from the barometer of intensity, there is another important gauge of seriousness in moods. We sometimes refer to it as the "bouncing ball."

+ *Extreme mood swings* **from high to low for no apparent reason signify a problem that definitely requires professional attention.**

The diagnosis "bipolar disorder" (also known as manic depression or manic depressive disorder) is applied when this condition is extreme and long-lasting.

Finally,

+ **moods in which very irrational thoughts and feelings seem to be racing out of control also indicate the need to seek the services of a well-trained mental health professional.**

Chances are, however, that you are not suffering either of these serious conditions. For most of us, some degree of moodiness is quite "normal."

MANAGING YOUR WEIGHT

82. *Trying to Lose Weight? Go Figure! Is It Worth the Price?*

❖

Although an attractive and slender woman, Melissa still felt that she was too heavy. "I need to lose at least ten pounds," she told her friend Jean. "Oh, please!" an equally-thin Jean replied, "You look great already! I'm the one who should be dieting."

❖

The weight loss and diet industry is a complex, often confusing, and potentially dangerous multi-billion-dollar enterprise. It promises eager consumers a slimmer, trimmer, and thinner body. Ultimately, their purses and wallets are lightened more successfully than their deposits of fat. The scientific literature on the subject of weight loss is quite sobering and suggests that the vast majority of people who lose a lot of weight are destined to regain it within one to five years.

What are the predictors of success? What differentiates the happy minority from the overwhelming majority of unsuccessful weight losers? Some clear-cut facts emerge when you examine the weight control literature. First of all,

◆ **temporary diets usually don't work.**

While they may result in a short term loss of pounds and inches, as soon as the dieting stops, the weight and inches return because most people revert to their previous patterns of eating and activity.

What does the research literature suggest? How can you increase your chances of lasting weight control?

◆ **Exercise regularly.**

Simply walking twenty to forty minutes daily will prove very helpful.

◆ **Maintain a food diary.**

Writing down everything you eat ---- tends to reduce impulse eating by enhancing awareness of eating habits.

◆ **Limit the amount of fat.**

Recommended level: no more than twenty-five percent of total calories.

◆ **Eat slowly.**

It generally takes the stomach about twenty minutes to signal the brain that it's full. Thus, extend your eating time to at least twenty minutes and it will be easier to decline second helpings.

Other helpful hints include:

◆ **Drink lots of water.**
◆ **Eat only at designated eating areas and at regular times. (Never in front of the TV, for example.)**
◆ **Enlist the cooperation of family members and friends.**

To ensure success, these activities must become a way of life, not temporary patterns. In their book, *Thinner Winners* published by Rosecrest Publishers in Oregon, Roseanne Welsh Strull and Howard Strull correctly state that weight management goes beyond diet plans, and they emphasize an important four-part program involving: Attitudes and Personal Development; Behavior Changes; Exercise and Activity; Nutrition and Food. We will touch on some of these elements in the next five segments.

Societal values about what constitutes being fat are unrealistic and all too pervasive. The body types in advertisements and on television create an unhealthy illusion. The current mania toward stick-thinness is extremely unhealthy, if not dangerous. The body types within the family are a more realistic yardstick of what people should expect for themselves. Self-acceptance goes a long way toward reducing the behavior that leads to overeating.

◆ **Before starting any weight management program it is wise to consult your primary care physician.**

❖ ❖ ❖

(The next five segments are not geared to the treatment of obesity but are intended for people who would like to lose about ten to fifteen pounds.)

❖ ❖ ❖

83. Sensible and Lasting Weight Reduction: Part 1

❖

"Losing weight and quitting smoking are simple," Len joked. "I should know — I've done both dozens of times!"

❖

Why lose weight? There are many good reasons for reducing excess weight. To begin with, being overweight is associated with a number of health hazards; high blood pressure, diabetes, kidney problems and arthritis are just a few.

Weight loss often leads to decreases in blood pressure and can even lower serum cholesterol, thereby reducing the risk of heart attacks. Severely overweight people are clearly at greater risk for disease than their normal-weight counterparts and weight reduction is a priority for improved health.

How many pounds should you lose? Your personal physician is probably in the best position to determine your ideal weight. But even if you do not reach your ideal weight, losing some excess pounds and keeping them off will result in significant health benefits, make you feel better, and possibly improve your outlook on life.

Many overweight people have had the experience of going on some popular diet, losing weight briefly, but then regaining that weight as soon as they went off the diet. Think about it. By definition, when you go on a "diet," it means that you will go off it at some point. And it stands to reason that you will gain weight once you go off the diet. The well-known "yo-yo syndrome," also called the rhythm method of girth control, is a consequence of "quick-fix" or fad diets that are little more than cruel hoaxes.

What then *will* work and have lasting results? Scientific studies show that any sound weight-reduction program must be composed of the following two parts:

- ◆ **A nutritious and well-balanced eating pattern that safely limits the number of calories consumed.**
- ◆ **Life-style changes pertaining to food and physical activity.**

In short, you have to, on a long-term basis:

- ◆ **alter your eating habits, and**
- ◆ **increase your level of physical activity.**

Dieting alone won't do it! If a person who weighs 180 pounds wants to weigh 165 pounds, he or she will have to eat and act like a person who weighs 165, not 180 pounds. In Part 2 of this series we will discuss specific ways to change your behavior.

❖   ❖   ❖

84. Sensible and Lasting Weight Reduction: Part 2

❖

"I just don't get it," Diana complained. "I'm very careful about how much food I eat at meals. I don't go back for seconds. I try to prepare low-fat meals as often as possible. Sure, I like to snack some, but usually I eat very sensibly. So why can't I lose weight?"

❖

In Part 1 we emphasized that sensible and lasting weight reduction requires a low calorie but well-balanced diet, plus changes in lifestyle. A good weight loss program is based on *energy balance.*

Think of your body as an engine. Food is the fuel. Eating even a little more than the body needs causes slow weight gain because the body stores most of the extra fuel you take in as fat.

There are two ways to use up the stored fat: cut back on food (fuel) intake by eating less, and increase your fuel requirements by being more active.

◆ **Learn how to regulate your fuel intake and energy output.**

Let your body burn the excess fat while preserving healthy muscle tone. By intensifying your activity, by increasing your energy output, you will feel better and slim down more quickly than by cutting back on what you eat.

◆ **Settle into a routine of three meals a day and avoid snacks between meals.**

Your body will gradually adjust to this schedule and you will stop being constantly ready for food.

There are a lot of temptations out there. The sight or smell of freshly baked pastries, seeing a commercial on TV that makes your mouth water, or just being in your kitchen at home with its easy access to food may prove to be irresistible.

◆ **Try to reduce the number of cues that prompt eating.**

You need to take charge by planning and controlling when and where you eat rather than allowing cues in your surroundings to control you. If possible:

◆ **Eat at the same time and in the same place each day.**
◆ **Get rid of fattening foods you have at home.**

Ask your family for their support in this matter. Don't make excuses, such as "I keep candy, cakes and cookies on hand to be hospitable when friends visit." See this rationalization for what it is. In Part 3, we will provide more behavioral tips to keep you on track.

❖   ❖   ❖

85. Sensible and Lasting Weight Reduction: Part 3

❖

Paul was what we might call "an automatic eater." Many times he would snack on something while on the phone, watching TV, driving in the car, reading the newspaper, or when studying for an exam. Much of the time he seemed to be deriving little, if any, pleasure from the food because his attention was elsewhere. But the calories mounted up.

❖

In order to lose weight and keep it off, we have stressed how important it is to eat three low-calorie but well-balanced meals a day, to increase your activity output, to avoid temptation by cutting down on food-triggering environmental cues, and to keep junk food and needlessly fattening edibles out of your house.

Now we will provide more behavioral tips. First, let's emphasize that whenever and wherever you eat:

◆ **Make sure that you are not distracted by some other activity.**

Be careful *not* to eat while reading the newspaper, talking on the phone, watching TV or at the movies, or while driving your car. The reason is that you need to be totally aware of your eating. The more distracted you are, the more you will be inclined to eat. Worse still, you won't even really enjoy the extra food you are consuming.

You want to avoid habitual-automatic forms of eating. When you have a meal:

◆ **Eat slowly and make sure that you are seated.**

By concentrating on what you are doing, you will minimize the chances of old, bad habits sneaking in and causing you to eat more than you had planned. Let us emphasize again that the two most basic ingredients of sensible and lasting weight loss are to:

◆ **Reduce the number of calories you consume**
◆ **Increase your amount of physical activity.**

Don't be taken in by fad diets. Don't fall for those plans that dwell on one or two foods to the exclusion of others. Avoid magical thinking!

◆ **While keeping calories low, introduce variability into your diet.**

Don't stick to the same boring food every day. By the way, the importance of eating slowly is that you are most likely to become satiated and not want to eat more and more. In Part 4 we will talk about the thoughts and feelings that are an important part of learning to regulate your own weight. We hope that this brief series will drive home the fact that sensible and lasting weight control requires and involves more than simply going on a diet.

❖   ❖   ❖

86. Sensible and Lasting Weight Reduction: Part 4

❖

"There's no point in my trying to lose weight," Lilly said. "My grandma was fat, my mom is fat, my aunt is fat; it just runs in my family. I know that my genes are stronger than my willpower, so it's pretty much hopeless."

❖

We have emphasized that the two most important aspects of sensible and lasting weight reduction are reducing the number of calories you consume, and increasing the amount of physical exercise you engage in. We now turn our attention to the thoughts and feelings that are an important part of learning to regulate your own weight.

It's important to become aware of your problem thoughts and feelings and to learn how to replace them with more constructive ones. Imagine this: You're trying to cut down on fattening foods; one morning, without thinking, you eat two large chocolate-covered donuts for breakfast. How do you react to this misstep?

You might say: "Oh no! How could I have done that? I've blown it. I'll never lose weight. I'm hopeless." *Or* you could say: "Uh oh, that's more than 600 calories. Well, I'm not happy about it, but I won't panic. If I'm careful throughout the rest of the day I can still keep to my limit."

◆ **Thoughts influence your behavior in significant ways. Some will hamper your efforts at weight control whereas others will help.**

Another example of a typical negative thought: "I'm not losing weight fast enough. I'll never get to my desired weight at this rate!" Now consider this more sensible alternative thought: "If I lose weight rapidly I'm likely to regain it just as quickly. I'm going to take one day at a time, and concentrate on gradual weight loss." This is a more intelligent approach, and more likely to be successful.

Here's another typical negative thought: "I don't have enough willpower. I'll never stick to a sensible eating program because I'm too weak." Instead, teach yourself to say: "Hold it! It's not a question of 'willpower.' It's not an either-or matter. I can learn the weight-loss skills I need."

It won't help you to say, as some people do: "I'm naturally fat and always will be." Try it this way instead: "Even if I am naturally fatter than others, it doesn't mean that I can't lose weight."

You need to challenge these automatic negative thoughts. You can assert control and develop a more positive attitude toward weight control.

- ◆ **Watch out for feelings that trigger inappropriate eating — loneliness, boredom, fatigue, anger and depression.**

You don't have to fill the voids in your life with food. Next, we will talk about using mental imagery.

❖   ❖   ❖

87. Sensible and Lasting Weight Reduction: Part 5

❖

"It's amazing to me," Nora said happily. "I'd resigned myself to being heavy. No diet worked, and I felt like a failure. My doctor told me to stay away from the scale, but to try to live a healthier lifestyle. Now I never starve myself, but I eat healthy foods and exercise nearly every day. I look better, and I feel better!"

❖

In addition to eating three low-calorie, well-balanced meals a day, increasing your physical activity, using positive self-talk, and avoiding tempting foods and other stimuli that can trigger unfortunate eating responses, mental imagery can also be a powerful weight management tool.

- ◆ **Picture yourself in your mind's eye attaining your goal, over and over again.**

Repeating a successful mental image makes success more likely. If you practice picturing something in your mind, it is bound to affect the real situation. So, before going to a dinner party where there may be tempting foods as well as people who may encourage you to eat things that are strictly off limits, you can rehearse an image in which you stick to your guns. Visualize yourself deciding that some of the food that the other people are eating is strictly taboo. Imagine yourself turning away from these foods and feeling really good about it.

Take a few moments now to try out an actual scene: Imagine that someone is offering you tempting food. Visualize the person, and imagine the aroma of the food. (Before reading on, please take a few moments to conjure up the image as vividly as you can.) Now see yourself refusing to give in to temptation. Picture yourself earnestly refusing to taste the food. Imagine yourself walking away from the scene feeling proud of yourself.

◆ **Negative imagery can also help you.**

Let's suppose that you are looking at some rich desserts that make your mouth water. It's going to require tremendous willpower to avoid eating them. Now, use your imagination to the full and visualize that someone had vomited all over these delicious desserts — yecchh!! In this case, you would probably be able to say, "No thank you!" without needing any so-called "willpower."

Remember the two basic imagery techniques: *imagery rehearsal* — rehearse in your mind's eye various scenes where you avoid temptation and stick to your diet; and *negative imagery* — when your "willpower" is lacking, use repulsive images to give it a boost.

◆ **The basic ingredient of sensible and lasting weight reduction is the development and maintenance of an overall healthy lifestyle.**

Merely going on a diet won't suffice. Lasting weight-loss will, at the very least, require you to take these steps:

- ◆ **Acquire a positive mental attitude,**
- ◆ **Gain emotional support from others,**
- ◆ **Move around (exercise) more often,**
- ◆ **Eat intelligently,**
- ◆ **Learn about nutrition,**
- ◆ **Practice stress-reduction techniques,**
- ◆ **Avoid trying to lose too much weight too soon.**

❖　　❖　　❖

"SHRINKING" AND SHRINKS

88. The Difference Between Psychiatrists and Psychologists

❖

"Psychiatrist, psychologist, they're all head doctors, right? What's the difference which one I go to?" Phil was frustrated and confused enough with his problems already without having decide on which kind of doctor to see.

❖

Phil is not alone; many people don't know the major differences among mental health professionals. Even relatively sophisticated individuals often aren't sure what distinguishes a psychologist from a psychiatrist. As the old ball park sales pitch goes, "You can't tell the players without a program!" Let us try to help you "tell the players" in the mental health game.

Psychiatrists are physicians ---- M.D. or D.O. ---- who have graduated from medical school and practice the branch of medicine involved with the prevention, diagnosis, and treatment of mental and emotional disorders. Most physicians ---- regardless of specialty ---- go through more-or-less identical training in medical school and postgraduate internship, then specialize during a period of advanced training called a residency. A psychiatric residency is usually a three-year program.

Because their primary training is medical, few psychiatrists undergo in-depth, specialized preparation in psychosocial treatments, and those who do usually learn traditional psychoanalytic or psychodynamic methods. Therefore, the first line of treatment for most psychiatrists will be to prescribe drugs, or to put the patient "on the couch" for lengthy analytic therapy, or to combine drugs with a shortened form of psychodynamic treatment. (In the next chapter we discuss the three major types of psychotherapies.)

Clinical psychologists are trained in the art and science of applied psychology ⎯ the study of human thought, emotion, behavior, and relationships. A clinical psychologist usually holds a doctoral degree ⎯ Ph.D., Psy.D. or Ed.D. ⎯ from an accredited graduate school, has had at least two years of supervised postdoctoral internship experience in clinical settings, and is ⎯ like physicians ⎯ licensed to practice under state laws.

Clinical psychologists apply psychological principles to the therapeutic management of mental, emotional, behavioral, and developmental problems of individuals and groups. They are trained in diagnosis, assessment, psychological testing, research methodology and nonmedical-psychosocial therapies and treatment methods. While in most settings they are not permitted to prescribe drugs, clinical psychologists trained recently have studied psychopharmacology, and are prepared to work closely with psychiatrists or other medical practitioners when medication is necessary.

There are others engaged in mental health practice. Much therapy today is performed by clinical social workers, marriage and family therapists, pastoral counselors and others. It is our bias, of course, that psychologists are best qualified overall to deal with mental health concerns.

❖   ❖   ❖

89. The Three Major Types of Psychotherapies

❖

Nina and Sue were having lunch together. Nina was describing her first session with Dr. Long, her therapist. "What type of therapy is she using with you?" Sue asked. "You know, I have no idea," replied Nina. "Are there are a lot of different types?"

❖

Someone (who evidently didn't have enough to do) has determined that there are as many as 500 distinct therapeutic approaches in the current mental health market. Fortunately, this bewildering array is easier to understand by grouping the 500 into three basic categories: psychoanalysis, person-centered therapies, and behavioral therapies.

Psychoanalysis stems from the century-old work of Austrian physician Sigmund Freud. Emotional problems are treated through free association, nonjudgemental listening and dream interpretation. The patient's resistance to change and the projection of thoughts and feelings onto the analyst ("transference") also come into play.

◆ **The aim is to produce insights that are believed to produce corrective emotional experiences and lead to personal and emotional growth.**

Similar to, and derived from, psychoanalysis are a variety of therapy approaches termed "psychodynamic," which also emphasize early life experiences, the unconscious mind, and see insight as the mechanism of change in therapy.

Person-centered or humanistic therapy was developed in the mid-20th century by American psychologist Carl Rogers, who believed that people naturally move toward self-actualization, or realization of their potentials. This approach as based on the notion that a person can grow and develop in a relationship with a genuinely caring, empathic therapist who neither applauds nor censures, but acts as a sounding board for the client.

◆ **The person-centered therapist-client relationship encourages self-actualization and working out of emotional difficulties.**

Behavior therapy, and its more recent derivative cognitive-behavior therapy (CBT), teaches people specific procedures, emphasizing what to do about current problems, rather than dwelling on past experiences.

◆ **The emphasis in behavioral therapies is on unlearning old habits and learning or relearning more adaptive responses.**

CBT tends to be short-term, solution-focused and goal-oriented. CBT also has a deep appreciation for the patient-therapist relationship, and sees it as the soil in which the specific techniques take root.

Today, many therapists draw in their practices on methods from several schools of thought. Such a flexible approach to client needs is sometimes called "eclectic" or "integrative" or "multimodal."

◆ **The best therapists base their methods on careful assessment of client needs, treatments that are proven to work, and an accepting working relationship.**

◆ **The worst therapists adhere rigidly to a narrow viewpoint, and do not adapt their methods to the needs of different individuals.**

◆ **If you are in therapy, ask yourself: Does your therapist fit you to the therapy, or adapt the therapy to suit your particular needs?**

❖ ❖ ❖

90. Short-Term and Long-Term Psychotherapy

❖

*Tim admitted that he was unhappy, confused and anxious. "Why not go
for some therapy?" his friend Joseph asked. "Because," Tim responded,
"I've got better things to do than lie on an analyst's couch for years."
"Check into it," said Joe, "my sister's therapy only lasted six weeks, and
I've heard that's about average these days."*

❖

Data from the National Institute of Mental Health suggest that about
52,000,000 Americans suffer from a significant psychological problem, but
that only eight percent undergo treatment. In other words, one in five
American men and women has an emotional disorder that goes untreated.

Chances are you know ---- or are ---- someone who fits the description:
people who experience stress at work, or suffer from low self-worth, or find
their marriages are troubled, or abuse drugs and alcohol, or are feeling
depressed. These sorts of disturbances are common among so-called
"normal" people.

If that's the case, why do so many people who could benefit from
psychological help fail to go for it? One of the reasons is unfortunately,
too many people still associate psychological problems with Jack
Nicholson's mental hospital patient role in *One Flew Over The Cuckoo's
Nest*, or Woody Allen talking about lying on an analyst's couch forever,
as in *Annie Hall*.

Very few people wish to be analyzed or lie on a couch for long-term
therapy ---- most people want *immediate* help with their *current* problems
and they want to spend as little time in a therapist's office as possible.

◆ **Effective therapists emphasize health instead of pathology.**

The most valuable therapy helps the client to recognize her/his strengths
and abilities and to make good use of their natural capabilities.

◆ **Modern psychotherapy tends to be short-term.**

When therapy is solution-focused rather than problem-oriented, it is
possible to make significant headway within a few sessions.

Some people avoid getting help because they fear that a therapist will
uncover deep, dark secrets. In a solution-focused therapy, there is one major
goal: "Let's see what is getting in the way of your happiness and is
undermining your personal effectiveness, and let's do so without necessarily
digging into your past and without opening Pandora's Box."

Short-term or brief therapy usually takes fewer than a dozen sessions to resolve a person's most pressing problems. During the course of short-term therapy, patients learn a general method of problem solving so that they become better equipped at helping themselves. It used to be thought that long-term treatment was superior, but recent studies have shown that short-term therapy creates less dependency and has many other advantages. Of course, some people are profoundly disturbed and do need years of treatment, but they are by far the exception and not the rule.

❖   ❖   ❖

91. Dangerous, Benign, and Effective Therapists

❖

Meryl had seen a counselor, but came away feeling worse than before she consulted him. She knew she could benefit from professional help, but her awful experience made her fearful of therapy. Fortunately, her friend Rene was able to convince Meryl to see a counselor with a reputation for being compassionate, caring and effective. Meryl was very happy with the results.

❖

It doesn't always work out, of course. Not all counselors and therapists are equal. Many are truly effective clinicians, others are essentially benign providers, and some are downright dangerous practitioners who actually do more harm than good.

In general, dangerous therapists are ones who steer only by the rudder of intuition instead of considering the available scientific facts. They tend to rigidly embrace a specific pet theory of human psychology and favor one or two methods of treatment. Instead of modifying their methods and theories to fit the facts, these "one size fits all" clinicians will try to squeeze the client into their unyielding molds. And if clients dare to say something that a toxic therapist disagrees with, they are told that, "I know what's best for you." As if the therapist knows them better than they know themselves!

Benign therapists are basically neutral, accepting or supportive clinicians who provide empathy, or a nonjudgmental relationship in which the client can explore thoughts and feelings. While better than the dangerous types outlined above, these therapists usually do little more than reflect back what the client tells them; they don't offer any concrete advice, direction, or actively help the client solve real-life problems.

♦ **Truly effective therapists usually approach therapy as an active educational process.**

In addition to providing an emotionally safe place to explore thoughts and feelings, these clinicians try to help their clients identify and correct misinformation that may be undermining their emotional or relationship success, and provide important missing information that was never learned.

♦ **Effective practitioners go far beyond conversational therapy and actively guide, coach, model and teach their clients to solve problems, feel better, relate better, and achieve goals.**

In addition to being good listeners, effective therapists must also be good teachers.

❖   ❖   ❖

92. Making Psychotherapy Less Mysterious

❖

Intuitively, Daniel felt that his emotional problems would not be helped by delving into the past. "I really don't think that talking about the second grade is going to help me now," he explained to his new therapist. "I think that in your case, you're right," she agreed. "I have a different course of treatment in mind for you. Let me explain..."

❖

In recent years, there have been major changes in the fields of psychology and psychiatry. One significant shift has been to make the process of therapy less complicated and less mysterious.

Many therapists now regard their work as that of problem solving. The old-fashioned idea of digging deeply into the past has been replaced, in many circles, by focusing mainly on present-day troubles or misfortunes.

♦ "Solution-oriented therapy" calls for active means of overcoming the fears, miseries, uncertainties, and relationship difficulties that lead many people to seek professional help. Moreover, this outlook lends itself very well to developing self-help procedures.

When you're faced with a psychological or emotional difficulty, we suggest that you take the following approach:

♦ Try to define the problem. Attempt to be very specific.
♦ Accept the fact that for the most part you learned to act, think, and feel this way, and therefore you can unlearn it.
♦ Devise a way to measure the problem.

For example, if you are bothered by disturbing thoughts, keep a notebook and make a check mark every time you catch yourself thinking in that way. Or, let's say you want to stop over-eating. Write down the exact foods you eat. Often, the very act of keeping score tends to lessen the frequency.

Problems are fully overcome only when we make a determined effort to solve them. If you continue to feel, act and think a certain way — the way that gives you problems — chances are that you are choosing to be that way when you could actually find out how to change it and make the special effort to change.

♦ If you do not get results, it may mean that you did not work hard enough at it, or that you are getting more advantages from staying the way you are. But it does not mean that you are hopeless. There are very few free rides in life, and effort is required to bring about change.
♦ Effective psychotherapy uses a combination of scientifically established psychological principles and "common sense" to enable people to live happier and more productive lives.

❖   ❖   ❖

93. Choosing a Therapist

❖

Hilda was in the market for a therapist. She knew that there are many different treatment approaches and many different kinds of therapists. "How do I know what's best for me?" she asked. "Shouldn't I have my medical doctor recommend somebody? Or do I just go see the guy my neighbor was going to?"

❖

Caveat emptor ---- let the buyer beware! Choosing a therapist can be a difficult and even dangerous task. Here are some useful tips for the modern mental health consumer.

There are a staggering number of psychotherapies and psychotherapists: no fewer than 500, according to a recent survey. Not only does the psychotherapeutic marketplace offer a bewildering array of therapies and therapists, but finding one's way through the maze-like corridors of the mental health system is difficult and often confusing. Because all therapies and therapists are not alike, people can end up in the care of unskilled and inadequately trained individuals. They not only may not receive the help they need, they may even be damaged further by the "treatment."

But what is the consumer to do? Ask a friend? A family doctor? Consult the Yellow Pages? In our view, the first step is to:

◆ **establish that the therapist is a licensed mental health provider.**

This can be done by contacting your state's Department of Law and Public Safety ---- Division of Consumer Affairs, or by simply asking the therapist directly.

We strongly recommend interviewing the prospective therapist by phone to ask questions about her or his training and experience, theoretical approach, areas of expertise, fees, insurance billing, and other issues that seem appropriate. Any therapist who won't agree to a five- to ten-minute introductory discussion over the phone may be too rigid or too busy to provide quality service and we recommend continuing to shop around.

When you meet with a therapist, determine whether he or she:

◆ **is warm, accepting, and non-judgmental,**
◆ **provides feedback and answers questions directly,**
◆ **seems flexible with time and scheduling,**

◆ is interested in solving current problems and not just concerned with exploring and understanding the past.

It is most important to emerge with a positive feeling of hope after meeting with a therapist. If your morale is lowered rather than raised, we recommend that you look elsewhere.

The way you and your therapist relate to and react to one another is crucial. If there is not good rapport, if you feel that you cannot trust your therapist, if you don't have full confidence in his or her abilities, or if you don't begin to gain hope that you will feel better, look elsewhere. It is your happiness and well-being that are at stake.

❖   ❖   ❖

94. Misconceptions about Receiving Psychotherapy

❖

"I'm not crazy!" Neil said angrily. His sister Emma had tactfully suggested that he might benefit from seeing a therapist. "I'm not suggesting that you are," she firmly replied. "If your feet hurt you'd see a podiatrist. For your depression you need to see a psychotherapist."

❖

Our society has come a long way in recognizing the value of consulting psychologists, psychiatrists and other qualified mental health workers for help with emotional problems, but we still have a very long way to go.

There still is a stigma about needing or undergoing psychotherapy. If it became known that a candidate for President of the United States had undergone treatment for anxiety or depression, this would undoubtedly be used against him or her. The unfortunately all-too-common attitude is, "Anyone who couldn't solve his or her hang-ups without outside help is too weak and unpredictable to be trusted to handle big-league responsibilities."

There is also a widespread (false) belief that psychological difficulties imply a generalized tendency for a lifetime of instability.

Consequently, whenever people who hold high offices in government or industry go to someone for psychotherapy, they often use false names, park several blocks away from the therapist's office, prefer appointments after dark, pay with cash, and cover up their tracks in other ways.

Because of the stigma, many who could benefit from help avoid it like the plague. It has been argued that as a result, many people in high offices are seriously disturbed because they have never received the treatment that they require. The truth is:

◆ **Everyone has certain emotional problems.**

Life is too complicated to escape having some psychological and emotional worries. Unfortunately, these normal difficulties are often incorrectly called "mental illnesses," which makes them sound ominous.

◆ **Most psychological disorders are *problems* and not *illnesses*.**
◆ **The notion of someone being "sick" or "crazy" is based on ignorance.**
◆ **The people who need help the most are often least likely to go for it.**

The truth is that people are too close to their own difficulties to see them clearly enough to make accurate assessments. Imagine trying to look at yourself in a mirror with your nose one inch from the surface. Everything works, the mirror is reflecting your image, your eyes and brain are perceiving the stimulus, but you still can't bring it into focus because you're just *too close to see things clearly*. To bring the picture into clearer focus, you'll need to take a step back. Similarly,

◆ **an outside (preferably trained) observer is in a far better position to pinpoint the troublesome issues in a person's life and offer help in finding constructive alternatives.**

We discuss this in the segment "Excuses for Avoiding Psychotherapy," Chapter 99.

❖   ❖   ❖

95. Therapy Is a Bio-Psycho-Social Process

❖

Smiling, Janice left her office for the day. Her last patient, a young man named Quinn, was overjoyed that he had been able to overcome his extreme fear of speaking in front of groups. "My presentation was awesome!" he'd said. "I bet I'll get a promotion!" Unfortunately, in Janice's focus on Quinn's phobia she'd overlooked his inability to have a successful love relationship.

❖

The current state-of-the-art-and-science views mental health and most psychological and psychiatric problems as *biopsychosocial* phenomena.

In plain language, this means that

◆ **the majority of emotional difficulties stem from three interrelated factors: *biological components,* such as medical illnesses and metabolic conditions; *psychological components,* such as thoughts, moods, and actions; and *social components,* such as interpersonal relationships and other environmental circumstances.**

This is very important from a clinical standpoint because, unless a therapist has this three-part perspective on the landscape of therapy, he or she will be likely to miss crucial elements that are necessary for success or lasting improvement.

This doesn't mean that all therapists must be equal parts medical doctor, psychologist, and sociologist to be truly effective clinicians, but it does mean that they need a broad and fairly comprehensive knowledge base that includes at least some medical understanding, a healthy measure of social comprehension, and a great deal of psychological training.

This also doesn't mean that all clients will invariably have significant components of all three factors to their problems. But:

◆ **unless the therapist makes it a point to explore at least the possibility of biological, psychological, and social components, critical information or important therapeutic directions may never be discovered.**

Unfortunately for the consumer, many therapists lack a broad-spectrum approach when evaluating and treating their client's problems. Instead of looking at their clients with a panoramic lens, many clinicians have tunnel vision and tend to reduce human difficulties to over-simplified labels and diagnostic categories.

The fact is that

◆ **therapists don't treat illnesses or conditions — they treat** *people.*

At least, that's what they are supposed to do. And people are all unique and complex and require a broad-based, customized therapeutic approach that considers at the very least biological, psychological, and social or environmental factors.

As a final note for this section, let us repeat our suggestion in Chapter 93 regarding the selection of a therapist:

◆ **If in general, your contacts with a therapist do not lead to your feeling more hopeful, go elsewhere.**

❖   ❖   ❖

96. *Psychiatric Medications*

❖

Virginia was seeing a counselor who diagnosed her as having a major depressive illness. This type of condition most often responds well to medication, and the counselor recommended one of the new anti-depressant medications. But Virginia steadfastly refused to even consider this route. "I never take drugs," she asserted, "not even an aspirin if I have a headache."

❖

While many people still hold on to myths and misconceptions about mental illness, more and more are learning the facts about psychological conditions such as clinical depression and anxiety disorders. At the same time there is increasing awareness of psychiatric drugs, also called "psychotropic medications." Psychotropic literally means "mind turning;" these compounds are used to turn a patient's mind from a disturbed or troubled direction toward greater health and balance.

Despite their safety, effectiveness, and tolerability, many people still fear these drugs, mistakenly believing that they're all addictive, or worse, turn people into drooling zombies! Such misconceptions may stem from reported side effects of the drugs, or from media images created by films or sensationalized news reports.

Matching the person to the right medication may take time. It's necessary first to do a careful diagnosis to determine if the emotional disorder has its origin in a chemical imbalance in the patient, and then to find the right chemical agent to restore balance.

Chemical considerations aside, there are three general categories of patients with respect to the question of using these drugs. The first group are people who are essentially functioning well and have nothing more serious than some relationship problems or minor stress-related concerns. These people are not candidates for drug therapy, nor should medication be prescribed for them.

The second group includes people with more moderate symptoms or problems. These folks may have some trouble functioning at work, at home, or in social situations. They may have various physical symptoms stemming from anxiety or depression. While they may not require medication and can be helped with psychosocial therapy alone, jump-starting the process with an appropriate chemical catalyst may be desirable.

The last group includes people who absolutely require psychotropics. These are people who suffer from serious symptoms — often biochemical in nature — that markedly disrupt all spheres of their lives. Without appropriate medication, these people simply cannot be helped.

♦ **Properly prescribed psychotropic medications are safe, and play a necessary role in mental health treatment.**

The main issues are these: Is the condition due to a chemical imbalance? If drugs are needed, what class of drug is called for? How can medications most safely and effectively be prescribed?

❖   ❖   ❖

97. Got a Problem? Take Something for It?
Or Do Something about It?

❖

Gavin often felt anxious, but was able to temporarily soothe his feelings of tension and discomfort by immediately taking a tranquilizer. "Thank God for these pills!" he often said, "I don't know what I'd do without them!" Lately, however, it seemed that he needed the pills more and more often.

❖

Broadly speaking, when people are troubled by emotional or psychological difficulties they have three choices for treatment. They can *take something* for the problem, *do something* about the problem, or *do both* — take something for it and do something about it.

For example, a person suffering from anxiety or depression can take something for the problem (such as psychotropic medication), or do something about it (such as a program of cognitive-behavior therapy), which involves learning new skills and developing emotionally healthy behavior patterns.

Gavin sought help from his family doctor, and was told his blood pressure was high and he could either start using an anti-hypertensive medication to bring it down, or he could lose ten pounds, eliminate salt and excess fat from his diet, start on a program of consistent aerobic exercise, seek ways to reduce stress on the job, and practice relaxation regularly.

In other words, Gavin's doctor told him he could either *take something* for his high blood pressure, or he could *do something* about it — a choice between *physical medicine* and *behavioral medicine*. Gavin could use the medicine until he lost weight and cultivated the healthy lifestyle patterns, and then the drugs could be discontinued, or at least reduced.

Traditional physical medicine emphasizes drugs; behavioral medicine involves lifestyle changes, such as developing new, health-promoting patterns of behavior. One of the most common and effective approaches to behavioral medicine is called "cognitive-behavior therapy." A blending of both medical and behavioral methods is often the best course of action. The resulting synergy may produce results greater than just "the sum of the parts." Thus,

◆ **the appropriate use of medication coupled with effective cognitive-behavior therapy often results in a curative effect that is greater than the sum of the individual treatments.**

❖   ❖   ❖

98. Connections Between Physical and Mental Health

❖

"I am not a hypochondriac!" Shondra asserted to her daughter Donna. "The women in our family just aren't very strong. You just better count yourself lucky that you don't have the health problems I do. I only wish I could find a doctor that could figure out what's wrong with me instead of insisting that it's all in my head!"

❖

The connection between mental and physical health has been written about for 2,000 years, but scientific evidence for a close association among emotions, personality and physical health has only been discovered during the past few decades.

Few would argue against the claim that many physical illnesses have significant psychological components. For example, people have been known to go totally blind after undergoing a psychological trauma; this blindness is called "functional" because doctors can find absolutely nothing physical or medical to account for it.

People who are anxious or depressed often develop physical or medical problems.

◆ **About half of the organic illnesses that patients complain about have psychological factors among the basic causes.**

Studies that examine the connection between depression and anxiety and health-related issues have not received as much attention as the relationship between hostility, anger and health.

◆ **A considerable amount of new evidence suggests that all three types of negative emotions — anger, anxiety and depression — play a significant role in physical health.**

The relationship between hostility, anger and health is well documented. Hostility is regarded as a toxic element that often is associated with coronary artery disease, and some researchers have found it to be related to other health problems, such as arthritis and asthma.

Research has clearly shown that there is a high prevalence of depression among medical patients, as well as a high prevalence of medical disorders among depressed patients. "Which comes first" is not entirely clear. Are people depressed because they are medically ill, or medically ill because they are depressed?

Anxious people seem to have many more health problems than their less anxious counterparts. It is believed that hypochondriacs are most likely to be anxious, depressed and/or hostile. People who score high on neuroticism tests often falsely report having physical illnesses, but there is also a strong association between chronic negative emotions and actual physical illnesses.

The point is, that with proper treatment, most of these factors can be changed.

◆ **People who are reluctant to seek help usually suffer needlessly.** And we think this is a shame.

❖ ❖ ❖

99. *Excuses for Avoiding Psychotherapy*

❖

Jason prided himself on his independence. "I've taken care of myself all my life," he proclaimed, "I'm not about to start now having some shrink tell me what to do or how to act. I'll get over this sooner or later; after all, who knows me better than **me***?"*

❖

We often find that the people who are most in need of psychological help are inclined to avoid it. "Nothing wrong with me!" they proclaim. "I don't need to see a shrink. I'm not crazy." In the vast majority of cases the need for psychotherapy has little (if anything) to do with "being crazy" (although a few people who resist treatment are in fact seriously disturbed).

Our society encourages people to be independent and autonomous. Consequently, many are unwilling to turn to someone else or to seek professional help when misery or anxiety take over. They believe that people with strong character can get over psychological difficulties by themselves and have little need for professional therapists.

Many people believe that they should not confide intimate or personal matters to anyone ⸺ except perhaps to a very close family member. Others think that emotional difficulties tend to work out by themselves. We've heard people say that if you just stop dwelling on or thinking about personal worries or concerns, they will go away. The truth is that by sweeping things under the rug, all you get is a dirty rug. It doesn't solve anything, and the situation may get worse.

Unfortunately, there are still many who think that to see a psychologist, psychiatrist, or other mental health professional carries a burden of shame.

It is also unfortunate that many tend to believe that there is something admirable in those who are determined to cope with their problems, conflicts or anxieties without seeking help. After unsuccessfully struggling to solve problems for years, desperation eventually may drive such a person to seek professional help. Such delays often make the problems worse, of course.

As practicing psychologists, we occasionally see such people. Often, all they require is a course of antidepressant medication, which usually turns their lives around in a matter of weeks. We cannot say this too often:

◆ **There is no virtue, nothing admirable, in needless suffering.**

Many people avoid seeking psychotherapy because they incorrectly believe that deep, dark secrets will be revealed. Today, most therapists are solution-focused and do not dig into the past at all.

❖   ❖   ❖

100. Narrowing the Gap Between Science and Practice

❖

"That treatment may have worked for the lady in your women's magazine," Janet's therapist said skeptically, "but remember, what works for one person may not work for another; I have to trust my intuition here. I think that if we stick with this course of treatment for a few more weeks, you'll see a dramatic improvement." Janet chose instead to find a new therapist.

❖

When there is clear-cut empirical evidence that a specific procedure works to solve a problem, we believe it is incumbent upon therapists to use that method first. If it doesn't work, other methods may be tried.

Nevertheless, there are still numerous therapists who ignore the data and insist on subjecting their clients to a useless "psycho-archeological excavation" through psychoanalytic or psychodynamic therapy, instead of implementing the proven methods of cognitive-behavior therapy. For example, there is evidence that insight alone will not help most phobic patients, those with obsessive-compulsive difficulties, bipolar depressions, panic disorders, and chronic pain.

One of the biggest problems in the field of psychotherapy is that practitioners often use methods that "feel" right, or make intuitive sense, despite the absence of supporting scientific findings. The result is that the *science* of psychology and methods of *clinical practice* often fail to connect. The practice of therapy is as much of an art as a science; there is room for creativity and innovation. However, when clinicians rely almost exclusively on artistry or intuition and ignore the scientific side of the equation, the best interests of consumers are rarely served.

Fortunately, some new developments are pushing mental health science and practice closer together. One such factor is an emphasis on *accountability;* more and more studies are pointing out empirically valid treatments for specific disorders. In addition, although it has many drawbacks, *managed health care* seems likely to promote science-based practice; managed care organizations are disinclined to reimburse practitioners who use unproven methods.

Perhaps an even greater force helping to narrow the gap between science and practice is the *increasing knowledge of consumers* and consumer-driven organizations like the OCD Foundation (obsessive-compulsive disorder), the Anxiety Disorders Association of America, the National Mental Health Association and others. It may be easy for lazy or unsophisticated clinicians to neglect scientific findings and work around managed care, but when four out of five new clients specifically request cognitive-behavior therapy, practitioners will have to face the facts and stop ignoring the data.

◆ **Don't hesitate to ask your therapist for empirical evidence that a suggested procedure is appropriate in meeting your needs.**

❖   ❖   ❖

101. Why Many People Don't Change

❖

Clive had enough money to pay for psychotherapy out of his own pocket. He'd been seeing the same therapist for over three years, but he had made no progress. Finally, his wife drew the line, "I love you, but your compulsive behavior is driving me crazy! You'd better find a therapist who can really help you with this, or I'm moving out."

❖

Why do many people fail to derive help or to change even after years of therapy? Many people believe that the purpose of therapy is to talk about their problems, rather than devising active means of solving these problems.

◆ It is not *talk* that is important, but *action*.

Poor chemistry between patient and therapist is another factor.

◆ **It is very important to feel comfortable with and confident in your therapist.**

If you believe he or she has your welfare at heart, and come away from sessions feeling better because the therapist's comments made sense to you, you'll make better progress.

There are many people who are unfulfilled and who seem to suffer, but who do not see themselves as having problems.

◆ **For constructive change to occur, it is important to identify specific problems, and to accept the possibility that something can be done about them.**

There are many people who say they have problems but who feel that that's the way they are and nothing can be done about it.

◆ **For change to occur, there must be a desire to change.**

Again, there are many people who say they have problems and who acknowledge the possibility of change but who seem uninterested in changing. The fact is that like any other form of learning and development,

◆ **psychological growth and emotional re-education calls for active participation on the part of the learner.**

Modern psychotherapy is a learning-based activity. If we are to unlearn bad habits and acquire new and helpful patterns, it is much like attaining any other skill.

◆ **Growth and change require effort and practice.**

The old-fashioned idea of simply lying on a couch and talking has been replaced by examining explicit problems and finding specific solutions. If people come for therapy wanting only to talk, and are unwilling to carry out homework assignments between sessions, change will be unlikely.

❖   ❖   ❖

102. Should You "Tough It Out"?

❖

"I can't stand whiners," Anne stated firmly. She believed in "keeping a stiff upper lip," never complained to anyone when she was ill, upset, or otherwise distressed, and always kept her feelings to herself. But Anne became extremely depressed after the breakup of her abusive second marriage. Her dreams and expectations had been shattered.

❖

Is it advisable to act so tough? Like virtually all extremes, this one is just as unhealthy as being an incessant grouch or a constant complainer.

Anne eventually had to move back to her home state of New Jersey and had difficulty finding a job, which made matters worse. An associate advised her to consult a therapist at a mental health center, or at least to consider taking anti-depressant medication. She declined to follow his advice and decided to "tough it out."

Anne continued to suffer for over a year and admitted that she had even thought of committing suicide. Eventually, things began to fall into place for her, especially when she finally obtained decent employment. Some may say: "Good for her! She held out and overcame her depression on her own." A friend described her as a strong woman with admirable qualities. Nevertheless, we maintain that she suffered unnecessarily and missed an opportunity to rally earlier.

It is reasonable to assume that if she had sought therapy, not only would the extent and duration of Anne's depression and suffering have been shortened, but she might have learned more about herself and perhaps been able to better position herself for a career and happier relationships. There is nothing admirable about prolonging misery and ineffectiveness.

- **Asking for help when you need it is a sign of courage and intelligence, rather than weakness.**

It is particularly alarming to see people decide to "tough it out" when they feel fatigued, describe themselves as "down in the dumps," can't get going, find everything an effort, complain of fitful sleep. Even more so with those who experience extreme mood swings from high to low. These symptoms can stem from many conditions, ranging from hormone imbalances to clinical depression to low-grade infections. A thorough medical checkup is a necessary first step in assessing the seriousness of such symptoms.

- **Frequently, "toughing it out" or "going it alone" makes as much sense as ignoring dental cavities in the hope that they will fill themselves!**

By the way, help does not have to come from a professional. A good friend can often do the job, but that means you have to swallow your pride and ask for comfort, advice or guidance. This becomes easier once you realize that health and happiness are more important than pride.

❖   ❖   ❖

MORE MENTAL HEALTH MATTERS

103. What Builds Character?

❖

Andre, a very wealthy businessman, insisted that his son, Josh, work to put himself through college even though Josh was carrying a challenging course load. "He'll never appreciate his education if it's handed to him on a silver platter!" Andre sternly remarked when his wife suggested that they pay Josh's tuition. "I made it without anyone's help," Andre continued, "Josh'll be better off if he suffers and struggles now."

❖

There is a widespread myth in our culture that good character comes from sacrifice and suffering.

Jim and Carol are a case in point. Both from poor families, they had been married for ten years and had struggled to make ends meet. Thanks to hard work and some lucky breaks, they were now extremely well-off financially. But their two children were being raised according to the principle, "no pain, no gain." Jim and Carol were not at all generous when dispensing love and approval. "You don't get something for nothing" was one of their favorite phrases. They could have made life a lot easier for their children, but they mistakenly thought that to do so would only undermine their children's self-confidence.

Do you believe that suffering is really necessary to achieve the good life? Do you know anyone for whom this unrelenting attitude brought true happiness? While there's nothing wrong with hard work, few people are better off from suffering. Life is difficult enough without intentionally inflicting adversity.

Many despicable, bitter, selfish people have suffered and sacrificed all their lives. Many warm, kind, considerate and generous people have not experienced much adversity. While some people do learn and grow from hardship, suffering is neither necessary nor desirable to build character. The fact is,

- ◆ **exemplary role models build good character.**

Parents, teachers, friends, coaches, mentors and neighbors who reinforce desirable qualities and constructively correct less-desirable behavior are the keys to character.

- ◆ **It is most important to teach children a sense of responsibility, integrity, fairness, and the skills for achieving their potential.**

To demand hard work or suffering solely in the name of "character building" may instead build resentment and resistance. There's little to be gained by needless self-sacrifice and hardship.

❖ ❖ ❖

104. On Being Indispensable

❖

Harriet worked as an office manager for a busy medical practice. Although she was given three weeks of paid vacation a year, the only days she took off were national holidays such as Christmas, when the entire office was closed. "Whenever I have to take a day off," she said, "I come back and the place is a wreck. No one knows this place like I do." Believing that the practice could not function without her, she even went into work on days when she was feeling ill.

❖

We come across many people who allow themselves to be emotionally blackmailed because they think someone is indispensable. Jerome, for example, is a successful dentist who complained to us that his assistant was bad-tempered, surly, and often discourteous to him in front of the patients. We asked the obvious question: "Why not fire her?" He said she was a particularly competent assistant who knew exactly what to do during all procedures and that he was most unlikely to find someone else as good. Jerome thought he couldn't get along without her, so he was willing to put up with her abuse. Interestingly, she was offered a more lucrative job elsewhere and left him. What happened? Did his dental practice go under?

Not at all. Within a few weeks, he had replaced her with a polite, pleasant and equally competent assistant.

Another organization depended on Clarence, one of their administrators, to such a degree that everyone felt if he ever left, the entire establishment would go bankrupt. He had them over a barrel and everyone jumped when he spoke. He services were regarded as indispensable by the firm (and also by himself). But one day, after a huge argument with the president, Clarence quit. What happened? Did the business go bankrupt? Sorry, Clarence. It was inconvenient for a while, but they eventually hired a new administrator who proved to be far better organized and much easier to get along with.

The myth of indispensability runs deep. Many people like to believe that they are totally essential and vital, but in most situations, anyone can be replaced. Things will be different, of course, but life will go on.

We have seen many clients like Harriet, who prided herself on being so important on the job that she considered it imperative to put in at least a seventy-hour work week. "I am so significant that without my input, the company would go down the tubes!" Often these dedicated employees neglect their own health, their family, friendships, or any leisure for the sake of the job —— then are among the first to be let go when cutbacks occur. It is our position that

◆ **your first loyalty should be to yourself and to your loved ones.**

Isn't it strange that "I'm indispensable" usually means, "I'm indispensable *at work*." The fact is, that's the biggest myth about being indispensable. Don't kid yourself. If, heaven forbid, you drop dead, your friends and work associates will get over it and the world will go on. If indispensability exists in any form, it is in relation to *loved ones*. No one can truly replace you with your loving family members.

◆ **Put your own happiness and your loving relationships first and foremost.**

❖   ❖   ❖

105. Premenstrual Syndrome (PMS)

❖

Isabel went to see her family doctor after her husband complained that she was "turning into 'Dr. Jekyll and Mrs. Hyde!'" "It's this PMS," she told Dr. Marks, "I'm always so cranky before my period that I don't even want to be around me!" After explaining the physiology behind PMS, Dr. Marks suggested Isabel try an anti-depressant medication, which proved very effective.

❖

Not too long ago, it was widely taught that psychological factors were responsible for the moodiness, irritability and other such symptoms that often precede a woman's menstruation. "It's all in the head," they said.

Today we know that it *is* mainly in the head ---- meaning that brain physiology is largely responsible for the fact that 90 percent of women report premenstrual mood reactions. Feminists do not want female hormones blamed for women's moodiness, and yet there is evidence that hormonal functioning plays a central role, according to experts such as Dr. Sally Severino, a psychiatrist, and Dr. Molly Moline, a physiologist at Cornell University Medical College.

It is not simply the woman's ovaries that cause menstrual difficulties. PMS mainly targets the brain, breasts, uterus, thyroid gland and adrenal cortex. The brain's neurotransmitters, such as serotonin, dopamine, and norepinephrine, interact with pituitary hormones and ovarian hormones and the end result is a mood shift. How this happens is still being debated and studied.

Nobody fully understands this process. Why do some women binge eat through their periods while others get moody and impatient? Why do some suffer with PMS one week out of the month whereas others become miserable for three weeks at a time? Why do some women just feel a little blue, whereas others experience deep depression? And why do about 10 percent of women go through the entire cycle with zero physical or emotional discomfort? We still do not have the answers.

Nevertheless, there is evidence that some women who suffer from PMS have low levels of serotonin before their periods. Any woman whose PMS involves significant mood swings and/or depression may want to consider being put on an anti-depressant. Lithium ---- medication of choice for other mood-swing conditions such as bipolar disorder ---- is also successful in treating certain types of PMS. The point is, PMS is a physiological entity that can be treated by psychopharmacologists and other well-informed physicians.

Some feminists continue to campaign against the PMS diagnosis on the grounds that it is damaging to women, but many experts disagree with this viewpoint and consider it regrettable. If you suffer from PMS, a well-informed gynecologist should be able to afford you some symptomatic relief. We urge you to talk to your doctor instead of suffering needlessly.

❖   ❖   ❖

106. The Nature vs. Nurture Debate

❖

"If you were a troublemaker as a kid, then your kids will be too," Wayne told Frank. "Personalities and behavior are determined by genetics — just like whether they get blue or brown eyes." "I don't believe that at all," Frank replied. "If you treat a child with love and respect it has to influence his behavior — just look at the psychological damage child abuse inflicts! It's environment, not genes that make the difference."

❖

As our national awareness of mental health increases, the question of *nature versus nurture* often arises. Are psychological difficulties, like anxiety and depression, inherited, or are they largely due to environmental factors, such as early childhood or other significant experiences?

The answer to this question is, it's probably both. That is,

 ◆ **nature and nurture — genetics and environment — are inextricably intertwined.**

Both play a necessary role in the development of psychological disturbances and most medical illness, too.

Here is an example that may help to illustrate this idea: Henry and Harry are identical twins — basically the same genetically. Both inherited a stomach condition that affords less protection against stomach acids than most people. Henry is an English professor who likes his job and has good health habits, such as getting regular exercise, eating low fat foods, and avoiding too much alcohol. Harry, an air traffic controller, finds his job very demanding, eats lots of fast foods, often takes aspirin, and drinks plenty of alcohol. This, as you probably guessed, is the environmental side of the equation. Not surprisingly, although both have the same sensitive stomach, stressed-out Harry developed severe gastritis while easy-going Henry had no stomach trouble at all.

This same idea helps to explain some psychological problems, such as clinical depression. Just as Harry's sensitive stomach responded to his stressful lifestyle, somebody else's genetic predisposition toward a specific neurochemical imbalance in the brain can be triggered by stressful environmental circumstances, resulting in the symptoms of depression.

So, is it nature or is it nurture? We believe it's 100 percent of both!

❖   ❖   ❖

107. Caffeine Addiction

❖

Rich made the appointment with Dr. Fredericks because he was suffering from nervousness and insomnia , which Rich thought resulted from stress. Instead of prescribing medicine, the doctor told him to stop drinking coffee and cola. Rich thought this was oversimplified advice. After all, he thought, symptoms like his couldn't be caused only by too much caffeine. He was surprised and delighted when, after a one-week trial of Dr. Fredericks' instructions, the nervousness and insomnia stopped.

❖

For most people, the word "addiction" evokes images of white powder, pills, needles, crime, and vagrants staggering down skid row. Yet, every day millions of Americans ingest significant amounts of a truly powerful, mind-altering and potentially addictive substance: caffeine.

That's right. Considering our use of coffee, tea, cola, hot chocolate, cocoa, and many over-the-counter pain, cold, and diet pills, we seem to be a country that has a very heavy reliance on caffeine to get us up and keep us going.

The fact is that caffeine is a powerful drug. If we don't think of it as such, it's probably because we generally don't connect caffeine with serious physical consequences.

Well, recent research has begun to link caffeine with significant health problems, such as elevated cholesterol, and an increased risk of miscarriage during pregnancy. And for years now, many physicians have routinely advised people suffering from a variety of conditions, such as high blood pressure, heart palpitations and cardiac arrhythmias, to avoid caffeine.

Furthermore, excessive caffeine consumption has been associated with anxiety, insomnia, and panic attacks. And evidence that is now accruing suggests that even moderate amounts of caffeine, such as two-and-a-half cups of coffee or five cans of cola per day, is physically addictive and leads to actual withdrawal symptoms, including headaches, depression, and anxiety, when abruptly cut out of people's diets.

Not all experts agree that moderate intake of caffeine poses a significant health risk or is addictive. And we certainly don't want to raise the alarm that caffeine use is a national "drug problem" — unfortunately, there are enough of those already. Nevertheless, we have each come across people who complained of anxiety and reported great decreases in this unpleasant emotion when they reduced their caffeine intake.

So perhaps it's a good idea to

◆ **take a good look at your own caffeine use.**

Do you suffer from anxiety, insomnia, restlessness, or irritability? Do you think you rely too much on caffeine to get you through the day? If so, you might

◆ **think about decaffeinating yourself.**

❖   ❖   ❖

108. *Attention-deficit Hyperactivity Disorder*

❖

For Casey, getting through high school was a major struggle. Although he knew he was smart, he just couldn't seem to stay focused and ended up doing poorly in his classes. Now, trying to cope with the "real world" by holding down a job seemed impossible to him.

❖

Everyone has occasional trouble staying mentally focused and has moments of distractibility, forgetfulness, disorganization, and difficulty completing tasks. And, who hasn't had periodic problems with being too fidgety, too restless, too talkative, too impatient, or too impulsive?

While all of these problems are certainly part of normal experience, for some people they can be so pervasive and severe that they can actually prove crippling.

◆ **People who are seriously affected by seemingly normal problems with mental focus, restlessness or impulsivity may be suffering from a condition known as Attention-deficit Hyperactivity Disorder — ADHD.**

The condition affects children and adults alike.

At the present time three distinct types of ADHD are recognized: *inattentive type* where the major problem is one of distractibility; *hyperactive-impulsive type* where the main problem is one of excessive activity or poor impulse control; and *combined type* where both inattention and hyperactivity-impulsivity are part of the picture.

Only recently has ADHD been recognized as the significant *biologically-based* problem that it is. Tragically, in the past, children who were suffering from the hyperactive type of ADHD, were labeled as "bad" or "disruptive" because of the behavioral problems connected with the disorder. Other kids who suffered from the inattentive type of ADHD were often thought of as "spacey," or daydreamers and were mostly ignored and thus failed to get the instruction they needed.

Today, wonderfully effective treatments are available to those who are properly diagnosed.

◆ **In most cases, the therapy for ADHD is two-pronged, involving appropriate medication, combined with behavioral and social skills training.**

The medication allows the affected person, perhaps for the first time ever, to tap into his or her reservoirs of potential, while the behavioral therapy aims to help the person utilize the potential to acquire specific skills that, before the medicine, were simply out of reach. Properly trained professionals can make a world of difference to the sufferers of ADHD.

❖   ❖   ❖

109. Hypnosis

❖

Martha had been struggling with over-eating for many years, but when she mentioned to her mother that she was going to try hypnosis, her mother was appalled. "How could you even think of such a thing!" she cried. "I thought I raised you to know better than to do something so dangerous! Who knows what'll happen to you when they put you under? Plus, it's a waste of money — that stuff never works!"

❖

Hypnosis is, perhaps, one of the most misunderstood and controversial methods of psychological treatment. The myths and misconceptions that surround it and hypnotherapy mostly stem from people's ideas about stage hypnotism. The truth is that stage hypnotism is, by and large, a theatrical performance and has about as much in common with bona fide clinical hypnosis as many Hollywood movies have with real life.

The fact is that hypnosis is a genuine psychological phenomenon that has valid uses in clinical practice.

- ◆ **Simply put, hypnosis is a state of highly focused attention or concentration, often associated with relaxation, and heightened suggestibility.**

Contrary to popular belief,

- ◆ **people under hypnosis are in control of themselves.**

Hypnotized individuals would never do anything they would normally find morally objectionable.

Also, it's a fact that not everyone is susceptible to hypnosis. Some people seem to possess a trait called "hypnotizability" that, like other traits, varies greatly among individuals. To be successfully hypnotized, you must want to undergo the process voluntarily and also possess at least a moderate degree of hypnotizability.

Even highly hypnotizable people may not benefit from hypnotherapy, and single sessions of hypnosis usually do not produce lasting results. Often, a person will have to undergo a series of hypnotic procedures to reinforce whatever constructive suggestions may be given.

The suggestions given to people under hypnosis appear to be an important part of the mechanism through which the procedure works. While many people won't accept or respond to an up-front, direct suggestion,

- **under hypnosis, suggestions seem to get into the mind — perhaps through the back door of consciousness — where they often take root and germinate into important behavioral or psychological changes.**

The most frequent clinical uses of hypnosis include: breaking bad habits, overcoming insomnia, recalling forgotten experiences, and as an anesthetic for managing pain.

You can easily test the benefits of self-hypnosis. Simply sit or lie down and get comfortable. Then, close your eyes and take in a few deep breaths, slowly, in and out. This sequence places most people into an altered state of awareness in order for positive self-statements to take effect. In this state, say some optimistic things to yourself and picture some pleasant events. Even a five-minute session can prove very helpful to some people.

110. Self-Fulfilling Prophecies and Negativity Cycles

❖

Mike dreaded an impending sales report he was scheduled to present to the department. Although the report was glowing with profit and efficiency, Mike was convinced that he would make a fool of himself when delivering it. He was so nervous on the day of his presentation that he claimed to be feeling ill and went home from work. "This proves it!" he thought to himself, "I really am a loser."

❖

"Self-fulfilling prophecy" ---- one predicts an outcome and then inadvertently acts in a way that brings about the very result predicted. Usually, the term denotes the creation of negative or unfortunate events, such as failure or disappointment, or unpleasant emotional reactions, such as anxiety, anger or depression. And, because many of these undesirable outcomes tend to build on themselves and gather momentum, they often become cycles ---- what most of us think of as "vicious circles."

In most cases, these negative cycles start with deep-seated negative and irrational beliefs, ideas, or expectations about oneself, other people, or the world. Such firmly entrenched negative beliefs are usually the product of upbringing and previous experiences, and are often implanted by significant people and events.

For example, if someone grows up hearing from his or her parents that he or she is "stupid, " "incapable," "bad," or "unworthy," after a while the negative indoctrination will probably take hold and the unfortunate person will start to believe these uncomplimentary and basically inaccurate notions.

Once in place, these core negative *beliefs* start to give rise to a variety of equally uncharitable, irrational *thoughts and expectations* that take the form of negative self-talk and unpleasant mental pictures. In short, if you believe you're bad, you'll probably go around thinking bad things about yourself.

These negative *thoughts*, in turn, create a host of negative *emotional states* such as anger, depression, anxiety, guilt and shame. Naturally, if you're bogged down in bad feelings, it's difficult to do things well. And as a result, your actions may include social withdrawal, avoidance, dishonesty, aggression, and even drug and alcohol abuse.

The cycle continues: if you're *behaving* negatively, actual undesirable outcomes are likely to happen. Poor performance, interpersonal problems, and even failure, divorce, and drug dependence can result. And the occurrence of these actual, negative outcomes serves to drive the entire cycle full circle by reinforcing the very core negative beliefs that started it off in the first place!

So, what can be done to break the cycle of these negative self-fulfilling prophecies? The solution is based on *corrective thinking* and *corrective action*.

 ♦ **Corrective thinking aims to uncover the core irrational beliefs and replace negative self-talk and upsetting mental images with more accurate thoughts and expectations.**

 ♦ **Corrective action encourages people to master challenges by confronting problems instead of avoiding or denying them.**

❖   ❖   ❖

111. More about Self-Fulfilling Prophecies

❖

Alec decided to consult a therapist for some mild anxiety problems. Unfortunately, the therapist told him that his minor problems were "deep-seated" and would get progressively worse without intensive treatment. Alec came home feeling extremely depressed and anxious. "I guess I'm really messed up," he told his wife. "I had no idea it was this bad."

❖

Everyone is aware that we can talk ourselves into unpleasant feelings and events. If someone says: "I'll have a miserable time at the party," he or she probably will have an unpleasant experience. Dan says, "I know Kim won't like me," and when he meets Kim, he acts obnoxiously and proves his point.

Now we want to talk about a different type of self-fulfilling prophecy. It is called "iatrogenic." That means it is caused by a doctor. For example, a psychologist may tell someone that because he comes from a dysfunctional family, or because she is the adult child of an alcoholic, or because there was some form of sexual abuse, it is natural and fully expected that the person will carry emotional scars and be psychologically vulnerable and disturbed.

We know many people who were experiencing some mild or transient psychological difficulties who needed little more than some reassurance, simple advice, perhaps some social skills training, or a course of relaxation and diaphragmatic breathing. Instead, they went to therapists who messed with their minds and they emerged feeling helpless and hopeless.

The unfortunate part of negative self-fulfilling prophecies is that they set up a "mental loop" that keeps the despairing and pessimistic attitudes going. Even some of the popular self-help books lead people to believe that if they come from broken homes or dysfunctional families, they will inevitably become emotional wrecks. Recent research reveals a much more optimistic reality.

- ◆ **With the correct treatment, even people whose histories are traumatic (if not gruesome) can outgrow and overcome their unfortunate experiences.**

So beware of labels and try to realize that you can overcome most psychological problems.

- ◆ **If you learn coping behaviors today, you will be better off tomorrow no matter how upset you were yesterday.**

❖   ❖   ❖

112. Personality Disorders

❖

Ursula had been in analytic therapy for many years for her severe mood and relationship problems, but it had been unproductive. Finally, she sought therapy with a different psychologist who diagnosed her as suffering from Borderline Personality Disorder. "Your condition is treatable, but it does mean a lot of hard work on your part, and possibly psychotropic medication as well," her doctor told her. Relieved, Ursula responded, "I'm so glad to hear it wasn't my fault that I wasn't getting better before!"

❖

The vast majority of problems that may lead one to seek or enter psychological therapy are treatable with high rates of success. These include such problems as *Mood Disorders* like depression; *Anxiety Disorders* like phobias, panic attacks, Obsessive-Compulsive Disorder, and stress-related problems like Post-traumatic Stress Disorder; *Eating Disorders* like Anorexia and Bulimia Nervosa; sexual problems; and even *Psychotic Disorders* like Schizophrenia. As dissimilar as all these diagnoses are, they all have that one important feature in common ---- they are for the most part treatable problems that respond to specific available therapies.

Alternatively, two other diagnostic categories, *Mental Retardation* and *Personality Disorders,* do not carry as favorable a prognosis. These problems seem to be firmly rooted in either physiology and brain function (as is the case with Mental Retardation), or in the person's character (as is the case with Personality Disorders). The current state of the art and science has less to offer these individuals in the way of effective treatments. While it is true that some retarded citizens are educable and can be taught some self-management skills, for the most part nothing can presently be done to significantly reduce the profound intellectual deficits these people have.

Similarly, some individuals with Personality Disorders (PDs) have profound character deficits that no current therapy can adequately reduce. But, like some retarded citizens, certain people with PDs can learn some basic coping or self-management skills that may help them deal with the world more successfully. In these cases, insight-oriented therapy will do little to reduce these people's difficulties, whereas skills-training approaches may help. The essential feature of all the PDs is a long-standing, stable and enduring pattern of inflexible and pervasive behavior that deviates from the cultural norm and leads to significant distress or impairment in social, occupational, or other important areas of functioning.

Currently, mental health practitioners recognize ten distinct Personality Disorders: Paranoid, Schizoid, Schizotypal, Antisocial, Borderline, Histrionic, Narcissistic, Avoidant, Dependent, and Obsessive-Compulsive (which is not to be confused with the diagnosis of Obsessive-Compulsive Disorder).

In Paranoid PD the pattern is one of distrust and suspiciousness; in Schizoid PD it is social detachment and restricted emotions; in Schizotypal PD it is one of distorted thoughts, eccentric behavior, and a reduced capacity for close relationships; in Antisocial PD there is a pattern of disregard for and violation of the rights of others; Borderline PD is characterized by instability in relationships, self-image, mood, and dramatic impulsivity.

In Histrionic PD, the pattern is excessive emotionality and attention seeking; in Narcissistic PD it is grandiosity, need for admiration, and lack of empathy; Avoidant PD is characterized by social inhibition, feelings of inadequacy, and hypersensitivity to criticism; in Dependent PD it is an excessive need to be taken care of, submissive, clinging behavior, and fears of separation; and Obsessive-Compulsive PD is characterized by a preoccupation with orderliness, perfectionism, and control at the expense of flexibility, openness, and efficiency. (Again, the latter should not be confused with OCD — Obsessive-Compulsive Disorder.)

If all this sounds confusing, it is! Nevertheless, the system of categorization is helpful to mental health professionals as they attempt to sort the complexities of human mental processes.

❖   ❖   ❖

113. The Importance of Individual Calibration

❖

Tiffany looked great and was obviously thrilled with the results of her weight control and stress management program, so Nadia decided to give it a try. "I don't understand it," she said, dismayed, "I've been following the same program religiously, but I'm just not getting anywhere. What's wrong with me?"

❖

Virtually all introductory psychology courses teach that everyone is unique, but this important fact is often forgotten. As a result, we find all sorts of general facts, figures, and average statistics that often have no personal validity.

For example, everyone has seen the typical charts that list ideal weights according to various heights and bone structures. Usually these lists divide their categories into small-, medium- and large-boned individuals, but much greater fine tuning is needed because there are different degrees of big bones, medium bones and small bones. Consequently, the recommended number on the chart may be too low or too high for certain individuals.

Or, take those numbers that have appeared in numerous publications and purport to measure degrees of stress. "Death of a spouse" heads the list. The implication is that all marriages are the same, that everyone loves and cares for his or her spouse equally, and that, therefore, everyone will be equally devastated by the demise of a marriage partner. Unfortunately, we have probably all met couples where such an event would be a source of relief rather than extreme stress!

How about those diet books that provide sample menus? After studying a recommended diet plan, one of our friends remarked that if she followed such a program she would gain, not lose, two pounds a week. She was correct. When she followed that plan she gained weight. Her metabolic rate called for far fewer calories than most people require.

Similarly, in the mental health field, too many therapists have a standard regimen that they use on everyone. Frequently, a form of treatment that might be wonderful for someone else might be quite destructive for you.

- ◆ **A really good therapist will tailor the treatment to suit specific needs, rather than attempting to fit you to his or her preferred methods.**

Our advice is as follows: Nobody is average; everyone is unique.

- ◆ **Make sure that your personal and individual needs are carefully considered, including the foods you eat, the medication (if any) you take, the amount of sleep and rest you need, the type and extent of exercise that suits you best, and so forth.**
- ◆ **If something seems to be disagreeing with you, try to consult an authority who will individualize the treatment plan.**

Don't assume that a specific medication, a course of action, or a particular treatment has to be good for you because everyone you know thinks it's great.

- ◆ **Remember the old cliché, "different strokes for different folks."**

114. Two Common Mistakes in the Workplace

❖

Although he knew he was rather timid, Jim saw himself as smart, capable and well-liked at work, so he was puzzled by his failure to advance as quickly as some of his co-workers. Similarly, Andrea had a lot of confidence in her ability and thought of herself as a dedicated and hard-working employee, so she was very surprised and hurt when her supervisor criticized her job performance.

❖

Most people spend more than half their waking time at work. Those who are happy with their jobs and fellow employees are most fortunate. But many get into needless trouble. There seem to be two errors that we hear about very frequently in our practices. The first one is illustrated by the tale of Jim (which was alluded to on page 39, "Mistakes Can Be Beautiful"). The case of Andrea embodies the second one.

Jim is a very bright and creative person. He thinks clearly, is personable and has original ideas. He obtained a job as a junior executive and was eager to impress his bosses in the hopes of getting an early promotion. However, at staff meetings and in other work groups Jim rarely spoke up because he was afraid he would not be promoted if he said the wrong thing, looked foolish, or made a mistake. Consequently, when the time came for evaluations, Jim was described as "unimaginative" and therefore ended up not getting promoted. Jim's all-out attempt to avoid looking foolish backfired.

◆ **It is generally better to speak up, even if you make mistakes or say the wrong thing.**

Employers usually respect employees who learn from their mistakes. However,

◆ **don't act as if you've brought all the answers with you.**

(When you're the "new kid on the block," during the first several weeks, old hands may resent a "too smart" attitude.)

Now let's talk about Andrea, who did speak up at meetings and was given a promotion. She was now in charge of thirty people. But Andrea treated her employees as if they were soldiers in the army. She made it perfectly clear that she expected everyone to be on time, to observe proper lunch breaks, and not to dally around the coffee pot. She often spied on them. The people who worked under her saw Andrea as a source of stress and complained to her superiors. Andrea's mistake was typical of those managers whose expectations are too high and who cut their workers little slack.

Fortunately, she was willing and able to mend her ways when they threatened to fire her if she did not lighten up. Andrea learned from her mistakes.

If our clients are at all representative, it seems that most unhappiness at work stems from timid employees at the hands of demanding and indifferent bosses. Our hopes are that

◆ **bosses who read this vignette will take the hint and lighten up, and**
◆ **their subordinates will take the risk of speaking up!**

❖ ❖ ❖

115. Alcoholics Anonymous and Rational Recovery

❖

After years of denial, Bernie finally admitted to himself that he had a drinking problem. Following his counselor's advice, Bernie started attending regular Alcoholics Anonymous (AA) meetings, but was immediately turned off by the religious and spiritual emphasis of the AA process. He knew he wanted group support to help conquer his drinking problem, but just couldn't seem to fit in with the AA approach.

❖

Within the vast landscape of psychological and mental health problems, few difficulties are as widespread and costly as Substance-Related Disorders, among which Alcohol Dependence and Alcohol Abuse are the most common. Many social problems such as traffic fatalities, domestic strife, absenteeism, homicide, suicide, crime and medical illnesses, to name only a few, are tied to alcohol misuse.

Indeed, the cost to society is staggering, with estimates totaling billions of dollars annually. Yet, despite its pervasive and damaging impact, the mental health establishment is seriously challenged when it comes to offering effective treatments for alcohol-related disorders.

For many years, the best-known resource for treating alcohol abuse and dependence has been Alcoholics Anonymous (AA) which, much to its credit, has helped millions of sufferers. Nevertheless,

◆ **AA is not for everybody.**

Some research has estimated that more than half of those who enter treatment in AA quickly drop out and either relapse or find alternative treatments. Thus, the impressive success rates that AA boasts refers to less than half of the self-selected population of AA participants.

Perhaps the most commonly mentioned limitation of AA is its very spiritual and "one size fits all" approach that emphasizes relinquishing control, choice, and responsibility to a "higher power." Also, the rigid adherence to the twelve-step program works wonders for some, but many people who are grappling with alcohol abuse and dependence require a far more individualized and flexible program.

In addition,

◆ **it is extremely important to address the basic anxieties, depressions, guilts, angers and other negative emotions that often contribute to problem drinking.**

Unfortunately, AA doesn't do this, as their mission is to get people to stop drinking "one day at a time" and provides only a supportive arena to accomplish this goal, not the specific therapy that many problem drinkers require to ensure long-term success. We see many clients who derive much benefit from regular AA attendance in addition to therapy. Indeed, the social support, sponsorship, and camaraderie that AA provides is often an essential component of recovery.

In recent years, alternative organizations have emerged ---- Self-Management and Rational Training, and Rational Recovery ---- that like AA provide a supportive group process but without the spiritual overtones.

◆ **Personal empowerment, choice and responsibility are important aspects of recovery.**

Unlike AA, which encourages people to surrender themselves to a "higher power," RR and SMART are firmly rooted in the world of free will and self-determination and teach people to make intelligent decisions about the pros and cons of drinking.

◆ **There is no single approach that suits everybody.**
◆ **We believe that the support group process is an important part of recovery for most people, but it is up to the individual to discover what fits him or her best.**

❖　❖　❖

116. Self-Help Books: Some Pros and Cons

❖

Carol's eyes scanned the bookstore's shelves looking for the two books that her therapist had recommended. "This is ridiculous," she thought to herself. "If these books are so terrific then I don't need to see him and pay so much money, and if he's so great then what do I need to read these books for?"

❖

There is almost an unlimited supply of self-help books on the market and more keep coming out each week. Among professional psychologists, opinions as to their benefits vary. Some feel that they do no good, others believe they are harmful, and others are convinced that they can be extremely helpful.

From our perspective, it depends on the book ---- some are excellent, others are mediocre and then there are those that are downright dangerous. A few publishers insert a disclaimer that the book cannot be used in place of psychological, medical or professional services and that a competent professional should be sought if the reader needs counseling.

It seems to us that there are two main drawbacks. The first is that most self-help books use vague and general recommendations that do not enable the reader to apply their advice. The second objection is far more serious. Many books end up blaming the victim and making people feel guilty for having problems. Let's cite a typical example of the first type of shortcoming.

"Change the way you think about failure," is the advice in one book. This so-called expert goes on to explain that people who learn from setbacks and then move on are healthier and happier than those who don't. Surely everyone knows that! The question is *how* can one put this into effect?

Similarly, another self-help book exhorts, "Get fully in touch with your feelings." This author points out that we tend to cram so many activities into our day-to-day lives that we fail to get at the root of our true feelings. So he says we should get at the source of our psychological pain by studying our emotions. There are two objections to this: (1) getting in touch with one's feelings (whatever that really means) can often be upsetting rather than beneficial, and (2) the author provides no guidance on how to follow his recommendation.

Now let's mention the second criticism ---- the extremely destructive aspect to certain self-help books ---- those that make people feel guilty for having problems or even for developing medical illnesses. "You are in charge of your own life, " says one such book, "and you decide exactly what will happen to you." So even if one is in a traffic accident according to some of these writers, this was self-orchestrated. These kinds of false and extreme assertions are harmful.

We typically use self-help books to complement our therapy. Used in conjunction with counseling, certain books can be extremely helpful. If a picture is worth a thousand words, no book is worth a thousand sessions, but some can speed matters up by a dozen or two.

(It's worth noting that we are not unaware that this book may be subject to similar criticism. Nevertheless, our intent here has been to offer brief ---- "60-second" ---- discussions of a wide variety of psychological problems and their solutions. We've made no attempt to disguise our biases or to prescribe treatment for your specific problems. It is precisely because human psychological problems are so individual and so complex that we have often suggested seeking help from a qualified professional.)

❖   ❖   ❖

Selected Readings

In addition to the books that were mentioned at various places throughout this text, there are several other references that we recommend.

For a general overview of the entire area of psychological disturbances, our favorite book is by G. C. Davison and J. M. Neale (1994) *ABNORMAL PSYCHOLOGY* (Sixth Edition), published by John Wiley and Sons, New York.

In our opinion, the two best books on rational emotive behavior therapy are the revised and updated version of A. Ellis's (1994) *REASON AND EMOTION IN PSYCHOTHERAPY* published by Birch Lane Press, and W. Dryden's (1995) *BRIEF RATIONAL-EMOTIVE BEHAVIOR THERAPY* published by John Wiley and Sons, New York.

We strongly recommend the incisive and scholarly-but-popular book by M. E. P. Seligman (1993) *WHAT YOU CAN CHANGE & WHAT YOU CAN'T* published by Alfred A. Knopf, New York.

One of the very best general self-help books for overcoming bad habits is by J. O. Prochaska, J. C. Norcross, and C. C. DiClemente (1994) *CHANGING FOR GOOD*, published by Avon Books, New York.

Our favorite book on the topic of understanding and overcoming depression is by H. H. Bloomfield and P. McWilliams (1994) *HOW TO HEAL DEPRESSION* published by Prelude Press, Los Angeles.

A. Fay's (1994) *PQR: PRESCRIPTION FOR A QUALITY RELATIONSHIP* (out of print as this is written, but available in many libraries) is a wonderful book for anyone wishing to improve his or her marriage or enhance their general interpersonal dealings.

B. Zilbergeld's (1992) *THE NEW MALE SEXUALITY* published by Bantam Books, New York, is the finest account of male sexuality written to date. (Both genders can learn a great deal from this book.)

We also immodestly see value in our book *DON'T BELIEVE IT FOR A MINUTE!* by A. A Lazarus, C. N. Lazarus, and A. Fay (1993) which dispels forty toxic ideas, and the earlier book by A. A. Lazarus (1985) *MARITAL MYTHS*, both available from Impact Publishers.

We are also pleased that the book by A. Lazarus and A. Fay *I CAN IF I WANT TO*, first published in 1975, was reissued by Quill (William Morrow) in 1992.

Index

MORE BOOKS WITH *IMPACT*

We think you will find these Impact Publishers titles of interest:

DON'T BELIEVE IT FOR A MINUTE!
Forty Toxic Ideas that are Driving You Crazy
Arnold A. Lazarus, Ph.D., Clifford N. Lazarus, Ph.D., &
Allen Fay, M.D.
Softcover: $9.95   192pp.
Popular book by authors of *The 60-Second Shrink* and
psychiatrist, Dr. Fay, debunking forty common misbe-
liefs that can lead to depression, anxiety and guilt.

THE ASSERTIVE WOMAN (3rd Edition)
Stanlee Phelps, M.S.W., and Nancy Austin, M.B.A.
Softcover: $11.95   256pp.
New edition of resource that has helped thousands of
women realize their strengths in love relationships,
with family, friends, co-workers, strangers.

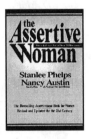

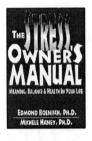

THE STRESS OWNER'S MANUAL
Meaning, Balance and Health in Your Life
Ed Boenisch, Ph.D., and Michele Haney, Ph.D.
Softcover: $12.95   208pp.
Practical guide to stress management with self-
assessment charts covering people, money, work,
leisure stress areas. Life-changing strategies to enhance
relaxation and serenity.

EVERY SESSION COUNTS
Making the Most of Your Brief Therapy
John Preston, Psy.D.
Softcover: $9.95   128pp.
Tight-budget times demand short-term, cost effective
procedures. This excellent guide helps you make the
most of brief therapy.

Impact  **Publishers**®
POST OFFICE BOX 1094
SAN LUIS OBISPO, CALIFORNIA 93406

Please see the following page for more books.

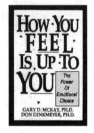